THE GOLDEN AGE OF
ENGLISH
MANUSCRIPT
PAINTING

1200–1500

THE GOLDEN AGE OF
ENGLISH
MANUSCRIPT
PAINTING

1200–1500

Richard Marks and Nigel Morgan

George Braziller Inc.
New York

Copyright © 1981 by Richard Marks & Nigel J. Morgan

All rights reserved

For information address the publisher:

George Braziller, Inc.
One Park Avenue
New York, N.Y. 10016

Library of Congress Cataloging in Publication Data

Morgan, Nigel J

  The golden age of English manuscript painting ..

  (Illuminated manuscript series)
  Bibliography: p.
  1. Illumination of books and manuscripts, English.
2. Illumination of books and manuscripts Gothic—England.
1. Marks, Richard, joint author. II. Title. III. Series.
ND 3128.M67   745.6/7/0942   80–12985
ISBN 0–8076–0971–4
ISBN 0–8076–0972–2 (pbk.)

First Printing
Printed by Dai Nippon, Tokyo, Japan
Designed by Dana Levy

CONTENTS

Figure I. The Westminster Psalter, London, British Library, Ms. Royal 2 A.XXII. *Christ in Majesty,* fol. 14

INTRODUCTION

The Gothic style in English painting began concurrently with fundamental changes in patronage and the circumstances of production of illuminated manuscripts. Until the end of the twelfth century, the monastic scriptorium was the major center for the writing and painting of books, although laymen were undoubtedly employed by the monks for some of the labor. During the thirteenth century monastic patronage ceased to be of such importance, and scribes and artists increasingly belonged to the workshops centered on towns. Direct evidence for this is admittedly rather scanty, except for Oxford where the documentation survives. Evidence for the shift in patronage is the change in the type of illuminated book produced. During the twelfth century large Bibles for the monastic community and scholarly works of theology formed by far the largest category of material illuminated. Although several important examples exist, books for private devotion such as psalters, were a very small proportion of the total production. Beginning in the late twelfth century, the situation gradually reversed itself until the personal luxury psalter became the predominant fashionable illuminated book. In the fourteenth and fifteenth centuries another devotional text, the Book of Hours, surpassed the psalter in popularity probably because it provided a structured reading program. This shift in the types of illuminated book also reflected the change from a predominantly monastic patronage to a wider range comprising the secular canons (especially the Augustinians), aristocratic laymen, and—from the fourteenth century—the lower gentry and the merchant classes. As the range of patronage widened, the types of richly illuminated book encompassed picture books such as the Apocalypses (Plates

10-13), Lives of Saints in the vernacular (Plates 6,7, Figure VI), Romances (Plates 35,37), and works on Heraldry and the Tournament (Figure XXIII). But private devotional books, the psalter and the book of hours, always greatly outnumbered all other types of illuminated manuscripts and provide the bulk of our evidence for the contemporary patronage and taste. In contrast to France, England had no strong tradition of illumination of secular texts.

It is difficult for scholars to establish clearly the centers of production in the thirteenth and fourteenth centuries. (See map, p. 32.) This may reflect a situation in which the workshops of lay artists and scribes were moved from place to place. Oxford and London were certainly centers, and there is also evidence of workshops in Winchester, Salisbury, various places in East Anglia (the main two were very probably Cambridge and Norwich), and also some production in Lincolnshire and Yorkshire. In the later fourteenth century and in the fifteenth century production seems to have been increasingly centralized in London.

The years around 1200 have come to be called the Transitional period, a transition between the Romanesque and the Gothic, when the type of painting cannot really be termed one or the other. The psalter produced for Westminster Abbey (Figure I) in the late years of the twelfth century has a style reflecting the Byzantinizing manner important in England since the second quarter of that century. Byzantine figures had at first been subjected to linear abstraction and idealization, but in the second half of the century, particularly in the work of the late painters of the great Bible in Winchester Cathedral, naturalistic aspects of pose, facial expression and drapery were emphasized. Byzantine art of the twelfth

Figure III.
Portrait of William de Brailes, Cambridge, Fitzwilliam Museum, Ms. 330. *Detail from a single leaf of the Last Judgment*

century, which had preserved classical structures of pose, composition and head type, acted as a catalyst shifting English painting towards the calm natural style seen in *The Westminster Psalter*. Influences from the Mosan region (the valley of the River Meuse in Belgium) and North France were also very strong in England during the last third of the twelfth century and contributed, with Byzantine art, to the evolution of the Early Gothic style. The production of the monastic scriptorium of Durham and other centers in North England towards the end of the century is a good example of the French and Mosan-influenced work. It was from that *milieu* that the artist of *The Life of St. Cuthbert* (Plates 1, 2) derived. In the lively narrative scenes of Cuthbert's life the painter conveys an intimate and small-scale atmosphere which is entirely new: neither is the monumental detachment and abstract formality of Romanesque art evident, nor is there any obvious link in poses or facial types with Byzantine models.

In the first twenty years of the thirteenth century there is a general trend away from clear-cut monumental forms (as in Figure I) to thinner and flatter figures, sometimes in mannered poses tending toward preciosity. The complete abandonment of any interest in Byzantine art is a prominent feature of the period. Head types no longer have Byzantine features or the characteristic gray and green flesh modeling. These changes can be seen in a group of six psalters most of which are connected with Oxford on the basis of their Calendars and Litanies. They are grouped stylistically around one in Imola (Biblioteca Comunale, Ms. 100), which was made for the nunnery of Amesbury near Salisbury. Other manuscripts of the group (e.g. London, British Library, Ms. Royal 1 D.X) have close links with an

Figure IV.
Matthew Paris, Historia Anglorum,
London, British Library,
Ms. Royal 14 C.VII.
Matthew Paris kneeling before the
Virgin and Child, fol. 6

Oxford workshop that absorbed artists who used similar systems of illustration but a slightly different figure style and coloration (e.g. London, British Library, Ms. Arundel 157). These manuscripts provide the first strong evidence for Oxford as a major center of production. A group of bestiaries dating from the early part of the thirteenth century which shares the stylistic evolution of the Oxford group (Aberdeen, University Library, Ms. 24; Oxford, Bodleian Library, Ms. Ashmole 1511; Cambridge, University Library, Ms. Ii. 4.26; London, British Library, Ms. Royal 12 C.XIX) has been associated with the North Midlands and the North by ownership or style. Lincoln has been most convincingly postulated as a center of production for some of them. *The Ashmole Bestiary* (Figure II) shows particularly well the mannered preciosity of figure pose achieved by elongation of forms and mincing gestures. *The Psalter of Robert de Lindesey,* made for the Abbot of Peterborough (1214-22) (Plates 3,4), and the closely related psalter also made for Peterborough Abbey (Cambridge, Fitzwilliam Museum, Ms. 12) show in a more developed form the new delicate small-scale figure characteristic of the Early Gothic style.

By no means had all artists *c.*1220 abandoned the blocky figure forms of the early years of the century. This archaic style characterizes a group of psalters probably produced in London (Berlin, Kupferstichkabinett, Ms. 78. A.8; Cambridge, St. John's College, Ms. D.6; London, British Library, Ms. Lansdowne 420). Likewise, the artist of the *The Glazier Psalter* (New York Pierpont Morgan Library, Ms. Glazier 25), working in the 1220's, still owed much to the art of the earlier period.

Figure V.
The Amesbury Psalter, Oxford,
All Souls College, Ms. 6.
*A nun of Amesbury kneeling before the
Virgin and Child,* fol. 4

William de Brailes is a rare instance of an individual artist of the thirteenth century who emerges as a distinct personality with a number of specific works ascribed to him during an extended period of activity. His name is found in *The Last Judgement* scene on a single leaf from a psalter (Figure III), and in a book of hours (London, British Library, Ms. Additional 49999), where he is described in the inscription as a painter. De Brailes' name occurs in records documenting the organized activities of scribes, binders and illuminators in Cat Street, Oxford, some as early as 1180, and there seems little doubt that he and his workshop operated there from 1230 – 60. The works which can be attributed to him are particularly wide in their subject matter, including large and detailed series of Old and New Testament scenes (Plate 5) and legends of the Virgin and the Saints. He is reputed for his skill as a storyteller and for developing the narrative potential of illumination. His workshop developed a form of decorative border in which the ornamental extensions from the illuminated initials formed border bars to frame the text area. This feature, most evident in two psalters (Stockholm, National Museum, Ms. B. 2010; Oxford, New College, Ms. 322), stands at the beginning of the elaboration of borders which came to dominate page decoration in English manuscript illumination in the later thirteenth and fourteenth centuries. A taste for the anecdotal in marginalia is also typically English and recurs as late as the Sherborne Missal (e.g. Plate 28). A contemporary of de Brailes, Matthew Paris, was a monk and chronicler of the Abbey of St. Albans for forty-two years. He also provided the illustrations for his own chronicles (Cambridge, Corpus Christi College, Mss. 16, 26; London, British Library, Ms. Royal 14 C. VII). The scenes illustrated are chosen with a marked taste for the sensational and anecdotal, and rendered in small marginal tinted drawings and occasionally with larger examples (Figure IV). Matthew also wrote and illustrated Lives of the Saints: *The Life of St. Alban* (Plates 6, 7) is undoubtedly by his hand and a prime document of his style. The technique used is, again, tinted drawing in which brown-ink drawings are partially painted with pale color washes.

The attribution of manuscripts using the technique of tinted drawing to Matthew Paris and "the School of St. Albans" is problematic and his role in English art of the thirteenth century remains controversial. Outline drawing was typical in England prior to the Norman Conquest of 1066, and enjoyed a widespread revival in the first half of the thirteenth century (e.g. *The Guthlac Roll,* London, British Library, Ms. Harley Roll Y.6; *Bestiary,* Cambridge, University Library, Ms.Kk.4.25; *Psalter,* Cambridge, Emmanuel College, Ms. III.3.21; *Roman de toute chevalerie,* Cambridge, Trinity College, Ms. 0.9.34). A St. Albans provenance for these works has not been established, and the tendency of past writers to attribute works to a School of St. Albans simply because of their use of the tinted drawing technique seems facile. It becomes crucial when considering two Apocalypses (Paris, Bibliothèque Nationale, Ms. Fr. 403 (Plates 10, 11); New York, Pierpont Morgan Library, Ms. M. 524,)whose provenances are analyzed in greater detail below. The iconography of these manuscripts is so similar that interdependence or derivation from a common model is implied. But, despite use of the tinted drawing technique, it is clear that they are by two different artists, each with a distinctive style, quite unlike that of Matthew Paris, and characterized by a

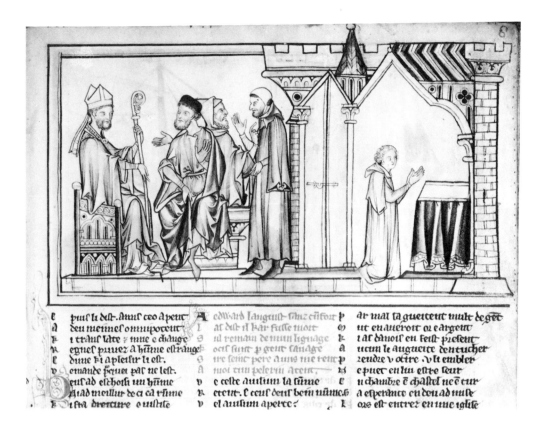

professional sophistication in contrast to his rather amateur, albeit talented, manner.

It is possible that the monks of St. Albans played some entrepreneurial role in manuscript production, and Matthew Paris, due to his presence there, may receive partial credit for the revival of outline drawing. But it should not be forgotten that the technique was historically common in England, and in widespread use among professional lay artists who were Matthew's contemporaries and artistic "betters." It seems more likely that he learned from them, rather than they from him. A "School of St. Albans" under the direction of Matthew Paris seems unlikely.

The role of Court patronage has likewise been obscured by the tendency to associate manuscripts of tinted drawing with St. Albans. The Apocalypses mentioned above are a case in point. Henry III's expenditure on the building and decoration of Westminster and on his palaces at Clarendon, near Salisbury, and at Winchester was lavish. Although it is difficult to prove that specific works of manuscript illumination were made under Court patronage, it is not unreasonable to assume that certain workshops flourished in the vicinity of centers inhabited by the peripatetic court.

The Pierpont Morgan Apocalypse has close stylistic links to the first few pages of *The Life of St. Edward the Confessor,* whose production has been situated in Westminster because of its similarity to painting once in the Painted Chamber in the Palace of Westminster. The Apocalypse may be an early work by the same hand. Further evidence for such production at Westminster is a series of five

Figure VII.
The Bible of William of Devon,
London, British Library, Ms. Royal 1 D.I.
*Frontispiece to Genesis: Coronation of
the Virgin; Crucifixion; Virgin and Child
with Saints Peter and Paul;
Saint Martin and the beggar;
a kneeling cleric,* fol. 4v

drawings, added *circa* 1250, to the late twelfth-century *Westminster Psalter* (London, British Library, Ms. Royal 2 A.XXII).

A group of manuscripts from the workshop headed by "the Sarum Master" (so-called from the Roman name of the town, Salisbury, in which he worked) is support for Salisbury as a center of production close to the royal residence at Clarendon. *The Paris Apocalypse* (Plates 10, 11), and *The Missal of Henry of Chichester* (Plates 8, 9), and *The Amesbury Psalter* (Figure V) have both been attributed to him. The style of "the Sarum Master" and his workshop seems to derive from the artist of *The Glazier Psalter* (New York, Pierpont Morgan Library, Ms. Glazier 25) and from the artist of a bestiary (Oxford, Bodleian Library, Ms. Bodley 764).

Although none of these Salisbury works can be directly connected with the Court, it is noteworthy that two psalters of the group were made for Amesbury and Wilton, both favorite places of retirement for noble widows and for education of aristocratic children. Henry III's own queen, Eleanor, became a nun at Amesbury when her husband died.

If *The Paris Apocalypse* (Plates 10, 11) can be added to the manuscripts by "the Sarum Master," two other Apocalypses of the mid-century, *The Trinity Apocalypse* (Plates 12, 13) and one at Lambeth (London, Lambeth Palace Library, Ms. 209) are more difficult to localize although both reflect elements of court taste. *The Lambeth Apocalypse* depicts, as donor kneeling before the Virgin, a Countess of Winchester who is perhaps Alienora, wife of Earl Roger, d. 1264. During its production, the artist came under the influence of a new style of painting derived from France, characterized by angular broken folds in the draperies.

Figure VIII. The Douce Apocalypse, Oxford, Bodleian Library, Ms. Douce 180.
The rider on the white horse, p. 13

A similar style change took place in the production of a copy of *The Life of St. Edward the Confessor* (Figure VI). The original copy of *The Life of St. Edward,* written and illustrated by Matthew Paris, provides the iconographic model, but this edition was probably produced at Westminster. The style of the artist in the early part of the book is related to the drawings which were added to the Westminster psalter, *circa* 1250. The drawings in the latter pages of the copy resemble stylistically the paintings once in the Painted Chamber of the Palace of Westminster, and reflect the French style that characterized those works. The text of the poem on St. Edward is dedicated to Queen Eleanor, although there is no evidence that this was the actual copy that belonged to her. But the taste for French art does seem to have been established at Westminster, and its popularity there set the fashion outside of court circles. In view of the parallels between the styles within the copy of *The Life of St. Edward* and the art produced at Westminster, and assuming the relationship of the use of the new French style to court patronage and taste, it is likely that this manuscript was produced at Westminster. However, not all of the work reflecting a French influence in this period is rendered in the manner of that associated with the court. *The Oscott Psalter* (Plates 14, 15) shows the angular broad drapery folds, over-large heads with severe facial expressions and angular poses of the French style, but interpreted in a more idiosyncratic and less elegant manner than that favored by court patrons.

During the period *c.* 1260-90 a long-lived workshop named after its most famous manuscript, *The Bible of William of Devon* (Figure VII), existed quite apart from the Court School. Textual evidence in the liturgical manuscripts suggests

Figure IX.
The Westminster Retable,
London, Westminster Abbey.
St. Peter

that they were intended for patrons in the diocese of Lincoln and the Oxford region. The manuscripts produced by this group of artists include *The Cuerden Psalter* (New York, Pierpont Morgan Library, Ms. M. 756), a psalter (Blackburn, Museum and Art Gallery, Ms. Hart 21001), a Book of Hours (London, British Library, Ms. Egerton 1151) and a series of Bibles (Cambridge, Emmanuel College, Ms. II.1.6; Oxford, Bodleian Library, Ms. Auct. D.1.17; Oxford, Corpus Christi College, Ms. 1). There were several artists working in a style derived from France, and it is very likely that some members of the workshop were in fact French-trained at the Johannes Grusch *atelier* of Parisian illuminators. Other artists associated with the William of Devon group are linked with the ornament and style of the de Brailes workshop (e.g. part of *The Salvin Hours,* London, British Library, Ms. Additional 48985). The style of the main workshop (e.g. *The Cuerden Psalter*) is characterized by stolid, static figures, broad angular folds of drapery, and border decoration with unusual long-legged birds and grotesque hybrid figures wearing pointed caps.

The "Court School" art from the time of *The Life of St. Edward the Confessor c.* 1260 until the end of Edward I's reign in 1307 shows an increasing similarity to contemporary Parisian painting. *The Douce Apocalypse* (Figure VIII) seems on heraldic evidence to have been made for Edward I before he came to the throne in 1272. Although the illustrations are unfinished and show work in various stages of completion, those figures which are fully painted show a mature form of the new French-fold style and pear-shaped head type with tightly coiled hair and beards. The work resembles, in its refinement, certain Parisian manuscripts grouped

Figure X.
The Ormesby Psalter, Oxford,
Bodleian Library, Ms. Douce 366.
Psalm 51, fol. 71v

around a law codex in Copenhagen (Kgl. Bibliotek, Ms. Gl. Kgl. Saml. fol. 393) and a psalter of the diocese of Meaux in Padua (Bibl. Seminario, Ms. 353). This French work is interpreted in *The Douce Apocalypse* with a strong element of the English style of the late work of *The Lambeth Apocalypse* and *The Life of St. Edward the Confessor* (Figure VI). The works in manuscript illumination of the last quarter of the century, e.g. *The Alfonso Psalter* (London, British Library, Ms. Additional 24686), *The Windmill Psalter* (New York, Pierpont Morgan Library, Ms. M. 102), and the sole survival in panel painting, *The Westminster Retable* (Figure IX), show work close in style to the Parisian illuminator Master Honoré (e.g. Somme le roi, London, British Library, Ms. Add. 54180). The artistic connections between France and England during this period, however, suggest influences in both directions. The figures become relaxed and sinuous in pose with softly drawn heads. This style spread from the workshops producing for court patrons to other regions, and is used by some of the artists of *The Tickhill Psalter* (Plate 18), a manuscript probably made in the diocese of York.

Late in the thirteenth century a series of manuscripts connected with patrons in East Anglia appeared. One group was connected with the Fenland abbeys of Peterborough and Ramsey (Plates 16, 17) and another with patrons in the Norwich region (Figure X, Plates 19, 20, 21). The period during which these were made extended into the 1330's, after which date there is a decline in quality of work associated with the region. The centers of production of these luxurious, lavish and sometimes mannerist East Anglian manuscripts are uncertain, but there is some likelihood that Norwich, Cambridge and Bury St. Edmunds were involved.

Figure XI.
Queen Mary's Psalter, London, British
Library, Ms. Royal 2 B.VII.
The Massacre of the Innocents, fol. 132

The chief members of the Fenland group are *The Brussels Peterborough Psalter* (Brussels, Bibliothéque Royale, Ms. 9961-62); *The Ramsey Psalter* (Plates 16, 17); *The Gough Psalter* (Oxford, Bodleian Library, Ms. Gough lit. 8); *The Barlow Psalter* (Oxford, Bodleian Library, Ms. Barlow 22) and *The Canonici Apocalypse* (Oxford, Bodleian Library, Ms. Canon. Bibl. lat. 62). The figure style in general terms is a less refined, more vigorous version of the French manner which first appeared in *The Alfonso Psalter* and *The Westminster Retable* (Figure IX) with relaxed swaying figures in rhythmic group compositions. An increase in the quantity of figures, animals and birds, both natural and grotesque, in the border decoration is particularly distinctive. An over-exuberance in anecdote and a lack of orderliness in design distinguishes the East Anglian technique of marginalia from its contemporary French counterpart. In the Norwich region group the emphasis on border decoration was even greater (e.g. Figure X, Plates 19, 21), and there was much more interest shown in this than in pages with miniatures of narrative scenes. Although there are several stylistic links between the Norwich and Fenland groups they differ in an important aspect: the distinctive Italian influence occurs only in the Norwich work. It is evident in the new technique of highlighting the draperies, the use of painterly modeling in the faces, and in more compact figures. This is first discernible in the work of the main artist of *The Ormesby Psalter* (Figure X) and suggests contact with painting of the school of Giotto. A second phase of Italianism occurs after 1320 in the added Crucifixion in *The Gorleston Psalter* (Plate 20), the now largely destroyed *Douai Psalter* (Douai, Bibliothèque Municipale, Ms. 171, known through photographs taken before its ruin by damp during the 1914-18

Figure XII.
Walter of Milenmete De Secretis
Secretorum Aristotelis, London,
British Library, Ms. Additional 47680
Alexander and Aristotle, fol. 17

war), and *The St. Omer Psalter* (Plate 21). Here the Italian influence seems to be that of the Sienese school.

The first third of the fourteenth century has been called the East Anglian period of painting because of the many important works associated with the region, but this categorization is unfortunate as much work in distinctly different styles is linked with other centers. The diocese of York is represented, early in the century, by the group around *The Tickhill Psalter* (Plate 18). Two large groups of uncertain location and dating from 1310 to 1335 are from the workshops of *The Queen Mary Psalter* (Figure XI) and *The Walter of Milemete Treatises* (Figure XII). In contrast with the Norwich manuscripts those associated with *The Tickhill Psalter* and *Queen Mary Psalter* are much closer in style to the contemporary French painting.

The Queen Mary Psalter, named after its ownership in the sixteenth century by Queen Mary Tudor, is profusely decorated with tinted or lightly painted drawings, both as framed pictures and *bas de page* scenes. The elegant figures with sweet soft faces are close to the Parisian art following Master Honoré and to the artists who were the source of the early style of Jean Pucelle. The most important manuscripts of the group are a psalter made for Richard, a monk of St. Augustine's Canterbury (New York, Pierpont Morgan Library, Ms. Glazier 53), a breviary made for Chertsey Abbey (Oxford, Bodleian Library, Ms.lat. lit. d.42) and a tract on the Mass (Paris, Bibliothèque Nationale, Ms. Fr.13342). The style of *The Queen Mary Psalter* group spread to East Anglia (e.g., Psalter, Cambridge, Corpus Christi College, Ms. 53, and a Book of Hours, Cambridge, University Library, Ms.Dd.4.17) and coexists with that of the Fenland and Norwich groups. The

Figure XIII. Wall-Paintings from St. Stephen's Chapel, Westminster, (London, British Museum, Department of Medieval and Later Antiquities).
The destruction of Job's children

workshop's most distinctive feature is its closeness to French painting, and this is evident, as well, in a rather isolated manuscript of the 1330's, *The De Lisle Psalter* (Plate 22).

The role of the English Court as patrons during the first half of the fourteenth century is difficult to assess. One of *The Queen Mary Psalter* group manuscripts (London, Dr. Williams's Library, Ms. Ancient 6) was made for Edward III's queen, Philippa of Hainault, and it has been suggested that *The Queen Mary Psalter* itself was a royal commission. Two treatises on government by the king's clerk, Walter of Milemete, were illuminated for the king in 1326/27 by a workshop of several artists (Figure XII), whose origins, development, and work place are not clear. It is known that they worked for diverse patrons and not exclusively for the Court circle. Most of the artists of the Milemete group seem quite apart from the East Anglian and *Queen Mary Psalter* groups, and they show few of the Italianate and French features so evident in the work of their contemporaries. Their figure style is characterized by rather coarse facial features and flatly painted draperies, although one or two of its members use more elegant styles (e.g. Figure XII). Like most artists of the time they are interested in elaborate border decoration. A few isolated manuscripts of the 1340's seem to make a transition to works such as *The Fitzwarin Psalter* (Figure XV) and the earliest examples of the manuscripts made for the Bohun family. Such transitional works are *The Psalter of Simon de Montacute* (Cambridge, St. John's College, Ms. D.30) and a Book of Hours (London, British Library, Ms. Egerton 2781).

The third quarter of the fourteenth century was not a highly productive

Figure XIV.
The Psalter of Stephen of Derby,
Oxford, Bodleian Library, Ms.
Rawlinson G.185.
Initial E to Psalm 80, fol. 68v

period in English painting, but there is one monument of the greatest importance, the painted decoration of St. Stephen's Chapel, Westminster, payments for which are recorded from 1350 until 1363. The Chapel was destroyed by fire in 1834 and the surviving fragments of the paintings are in the British Museum (Figure XIII). The primary source of inspiration behind them is, once again, Italian early Trecento art. The soft blues and pinks, the small *grisaille* figures in the niches in *The Destruction of Job's Children* and the architectural structures in *The Messengers conveying the news to Job* are particularly reminiscent of the art of Siena as represented by Ambrogio and Pietro Lorenzetti. Above all, this is apparent in the understanding of architectural perspective. No Italian artists, however, were directly involved. All the painters mentioned in the accounts, with one exception, have English names, and their representations of certain features (especially facial types) are quite un-Italian. Moreover, recent scientific analysis has established that the paint was applied by means of an oil medium, a technique which became current in Italy only during the second half of the fifteenth century. One of the painters, Hugh of St. Albans, has been identified as the Hugh Peyntour who in his will of 1368 left a table of "VII peces de Lumbardy," i.e. an Italian altarpiece or panel painting; it is, perhaps, through imported works such as these, that the St. Stephen's painters derived their knowledge of Italian art.

St. Stephen's is hardly an isolated example of Italian influence in this period. The artist known as "The Egerton Master" after a series of *grisaille* illustrations in a Book of Genesis (London, British Library, Ms. Egerton 1894) executed several other manuscripts including, between 1348 and *c.* 1382, a psalter for Stephen of

Figure XV.
The Fitzwarin Psalter, Paris,
Bibliothèque Nationale, Ms. Lat. 765.
The Resurrection, fol. 18

Derby, Prior of Christ Church Cathedral, Dublin. This psalter contains foliage forms, typically daisy, derived from those common in East Anglian manuscripts of the early fourteenth century, but its indebtedness to Italian art is demonstrated by the skillful use of foreshortening in the initial to Psalm 80 (Figure XIV).

"The Egerton Master" was responsible for two full-page miniatures in *The Fitzwarin Psalter* which are probably additions to this manuscript by another hand; the fourteen other full-page miniatures are by a different artist whose style is highly idiosyncratic, with crude but expressive figures. As *the Resurrection* miniature (Figure XV) shows, the scenes are dominated by their architectural frameworks. The closest parallels appear to be in such Flemish manuscripts of the mid-fourteenth century as those belonging to Louis de Mâle, Count of Flanders. The Lady Chapel windows of Christ Church Cathedral, Oxford, and the murals at Potter Heigham (Norfolk) furnish good examples of similar enframing canopies in English monumental painting of the third quarter of the century.

Both Flemish and Italianate elements appear in the largest single group of manuscripts executed in England during the second half of the fourteenth century. This consists of some ten books commissioned by the Bohun family, and in particular by Humphrey de Bohun, Earl of Hereford (*d.* 1373), and his daughters Eleanor and Mary. Among the most important are three psalters in Vienna (Plate 23) and Oxford (Exeter College, Ms. 47, and Bodleian Library, Ms. Auct. D. 4.4). A detailed study of the heraldry reveals that the date range for the entire group extends from before 1361 until possibly as late as 1399. One of the earliest appears to be *The Vienna Bohun Psalter* (Plate 23). Contrary to what has often been said, the

Figure XVI.
The Lovell Lectionary, London,
British Library, Ms. Harley 7026.
*John Siferwas presenting the
Lectionary to John, Lord Lovell of
Titchmarsh*, fol. 4v

group is not homogeneous and at least two distinct figure styles are recognizable. One, characterized by heavy outlines, thinly modeled drapery folds, and thick wavy hair (Plate 23), is connected with Flemish manuscripts. The other, characterized by heavily painted faces with beady eyes and thin narrow mouths, and by drapery modeled by means of white highlights, is the style usually associated with the Bohun group. This second style displays distinct echoes of the Italianate East Anglian manuscripts of the period *c.* 1330-40 and a general affinity with Lombard painting, but its precise sources have not been identified. The manuscripts also contain iconographic themes which can only have originated south of the Alps, notably the Virgin of Mercy and The Man of Sorrows. The second "Bohun" style lingered into the 1390's, as evidenced by Style C in *The Carmelite Missal* (Plate 26A). This manuscript will be considered in more detail below.

During the 1380's and early '90's another group of manuscripts emerged, centered around *The Lytlington Missal* of 1383-84 (Plate 25), executed for an abbot of Westminster. This manuscript has some affinities with the second "Bohun" style, but the heavy eyelids and high arched brows which often give a rather surprised expression are easily distinguishable from the facial types found in the Bohun manuscripts. The illumination was carried out by two main hands. One of them (not the artist of *the Crucifixion* page) can be seen in several other manuscripts, including *The Belknap Hours* (private collection) and an Apocalypse (Cambridge, Trinity College, Ms. B. 10.2).

Also closely associated with Westminster is *The Liber Regalis* (Plate 24), which probably just pre-dates *The Lytlington Missal*. It has become traditional among art

Figure XVII.
Masses and Devotions,
London, British Library,
Ms. Additional 16998.
Miniature of St. John the
Evangelist with the
"signature" of Herman
Scheerre, fol. 37

historians to consider this manuscript to be the work of a Bohemian illuminator in the entourage of Richard II's wife, Anne of Bohemia, or at the very least, to reflect the influence of a Prague artist. These theories have recently been discounted, and the origin of the distinctive *Liber Regalis* style has still to be satisfactorily explained. Five other English manuscripts can be associated stylistically with *The Liber Regalis,* including a royal charter dated 1389 in the Guildhall at Shrewsbury, and Hand B in the Carmelite Missal.

A variety of trends can be traced in English painting during the last two decades of the fourteenth century. In addition to the Italian-influenced "Bohun" style and *The Lytlington Missal* and *Liber Regalis* styles, yet another is represented by the *Apocalypse* wall-paintings in the chapter-house at Westminster Abbey. These murals probably date from 1395-1404 and are closely allied to the work of Master Bertram (*d.* 1414/15), a panel painter of Hamburg, a Hanseatic city enjoying strong commercial links with England during the late Middle Ages.

Most of the trends current in manuscript illumination at the time are united in *The Carmelite Missal.* Of the three styles in this large volume distinguished by Margaret Rickert, Style C (Plate 26A) is in the Bohun tradition and Style B (Plate 26B) is closely related to *The Liber Regalis* group. With Style A (Plate 27), English painting enters an entirely new phase. The miniatures by the main artist working in Style A display a sensitive pictorial modeling and a command of perspective without parallel in contemporary English book-illumination.

This illuminator appears to have introduced the fully developed International Gothic style into England. It is generally accepted that he was of Continental

Figure XVIII. The Pepysian Sketchbook, Cambridge, Magdalene College Library, Pepysian Library Ms. 1916. *Two apostles,* fol. 4v

origin: quite apart from his figure style and rendering of space, he used the acanthus leaf in his initial letters, a leaf form hitherto unknown in English painting. The precise area from which he came is still undetermined. His work has been linked, not very convincingly, with the northern Netherlands, but an alternative theory relates it to a group of manuscripts from the Ypres region in Flanders. The liturgy and iconography of *The Carmelite Missal* point to a date after 1393 for the decoration, although the *terminus ante quem* of 1398 suggested by Rickert is not based on the firmest of grounds.

Following closely behind the artists of Style A of *The Carmelite Missal* three *limnours* of outstanding ability emerged: John Siferwas, Johannes, and Herman Scheerre. They firmly established the International Gothic style in England and dominated book production for the first three decades of the fifteenth century. John Siferwas was a Dominican friar whose name first appears in 1380 and who probably spent most of his working life at a priory somewhere in the southwest. The testator of a will dated 1427 in which Siferwas is mentioned came from the district around Muchelney (Somerset). More important, the manuscripts which can be ascribed to the artist and his workshop are connected with Sherborne Abbey in Dorset (*The Sherborne Missal,* datable on heraldic and patronage evidence to 1396-1407), Salisbury (*The Lovell Lectionary,* commissioned for the Cathedral by John, 5th Lord Lovell of Titchmarsh, *d.* 1408) and Glastonbury Abbey, Somerset (a copy of *Stephen Langton's Glosses on the Pentateuch* in Trinity College, Cambridge, Ms. B.3.7)—all in that area. Siferwas's style can best be appreciated in the lavishly decorated *Sherborne Missal* (Plates 28-30) and *The Lovell Lectionary* (Figure XVI).

The voluminous draperies and gentle facial features of his figures conform to the same canons of International Gothic as does Style A in *The Carmelite Missal,* but Siferwas's style is quite distinct from the latter's. Siferwas employed stronger, harsher colors. His scenes lack spatial depth and tend to be overcrowded; the initials are frequently overwhelmed by lively decoration in the borders and margins. His emphasis on borders and marginal decoration, and his meticulous depiction of nature, owe much to the East Anglian tradition of the early fourteenth century. He combined these indigenous features with the new "soft" figure style to create a highly individual and attractive art. He may have come into contact with International Gothic by means of northwest German painting, for there are some iconographic and stylistic parallels with the art of Cologne and Westphalia around 1400.

The often stated assertion that Siferwas exerted considerable influence over artists of succeeding generations seems unlikely inasmuch as he appears to have been working in a region considerably removed from the centers of manuscript production. Some of Siferwas's contemporaries, particularly Johannes, used certain features found in his work, but none ever decorated an entire page in the same manner as he.

Johannes is identified in an inscription *Johannes me fecit* on the hem of the Great Caam in a miniature on fol. 220 of *Li Romans du boin roi Alexandre* and *Li Livres du Graunt Caam.* Some half-dozen manuscripts of which the finest are *The Alexander* (Plate 35) and *The Hours of Elizabeth the Queen* (Plate 36) can be attributed to him and his workshop. There are some affinities between the works of Johannes and

Siferwas, notably in certain facial types, the liking for portrait heads and a tendency to overcrowd scenes. Nevertheless, these similarities have been over-stressed. In their palettes and border decorations the two are very different. Johannes has a particular talent for imparting a dramatic tension to his miniatures by the use of lively, varied gestures and poses, and by strong color contrasts.

The third, and most important, of the manuscript illuminators working in the early phases of the International Gothic style was Herman Scheerre. His name and/or motto, *Omnia levia sunt amanti: si quis amat non laborat* ("All is easy for one who loves: he who loves toils not"), which appears to be his trademark, can be found in seven manuscripts. These include *The Chichele Breviary* (London, Lambeth Palace, Ms. 69), a book of Masses and Devotions (Figure XVII), *The Beaufort/Beauchamp Hours* (Plate 32) and *The Bedford Psalter and Hours* (Plate 34B). Only three, spanning 1405-23, provide any dating evidence.

Two London wills dated 1407 mention a *Herman lymnour* who may be Herman Scheerre. In one of these wills three of the people named are said to be from Cologne, leading some scholars to associate him with this city. They have identified him as the Herman of Cologne who worked there in 1388-89 and subsequently, 1401-1403, was an assistant of Jean Malouel at the Champmol Charterhouse, Dijon. Furthermore, it has recently been discovered that a family of artists named Scheerre lived in Duisburg, nearly fifty miles north of Cologne, during the late Middle Ages. Despite this evidence, attempts to relate Scheerre's style to early fifteenth-century painting in Cologne and the Lower Rhine area are not convincing. Comparisons with the style of Flemish manuscripts from the

Figure XX.
Select Psalms of Humphrey, Duke
of Gloucester, London, British
Library, Ms. Royal 2 B.I.
*Duke Humphrey with St. Alban before
the Man of Sorrows,* fol. 8

Ypres/Bruges/Tournai region are the most persuasive to have been suggested so far. Scheerre's connection with this group of manuscripts is strengthened by the fact that he collaborated with an illuminator from this region in a book of hours (Oxford, Bodleian Library, Ms. Lat. liturg. f.2) and *The Beaufort/Beauchamp Hours* (Plates 31, 32).

This artist has been termed "The Master of the Beaufort Saints," after his twelve miniatures in *The Beaufort/Beauchamp Hours.* When his miniature of *St. John of Bridlington* (Plate 31) is compared with Scheerre's miniature of *The Annunciation* (Plate 32) it becomes evident that indebted though the latter may have been to the Ypres/Bruges/Tournai tradition, he was not slavishly dependent upon it. "The Master of the Beaufort Saints" is slightly coarser and more dynamic than Scheerre in his use of paint, employs heavier, more strongly contrasting colors, and shows a greater interest in creating spatial depth than does Scheerre. Unlike Siferwas, Scheerre usually confined his illumination to the initial or miniature and employed a fairly standardized border design. His miniatures are delicate; faces are smooth, flesh tones painted with great sensitivity over cool green grounds; and draperies fall in rich soft folds with a subtle blending of colors.

The Bedford Psalter and Hours (Plate 34B) was one of the last manuscripts upon which Scheerre worked, although not all of the decoration is by him and his workshop. Some of the initials (Plates 33, 34A) are by an exceptionally talented illuminator whose use of landscape and starry skies reveals the influence of "The Boucicaut Master," a leading Parisian artist of the early fifteenth century. *The Bedford Psalter and Hours* is a particularly important manuscript, not only because of the scale of its decoration, but also because it is a collaborative effort by leading

Figure XXI. Founder's Charter to King's College Cambridge Upon Act of Parliament, Cambridge, King's College.
Henry VI (in the initial) with the Lords and Commons kneeling before the Virgin crowned by the Trinity.

illuminators of the day. In addition to Scheerre and his workshop and the master of the French-style initials, a third hand, an assistant of Johannes, painted the small Passion miniatures.

The International Gothic style in England during the first third of the fifteenth century was not confined to illumination alone, but was disseminated throughout all branches of painting, no doubt by means of artists' sketchbooks such as that in the Pepysian Library at Magdalene College, Cambridge (Figure XVIII). Of all monumental painting, it is in stained glass that the International Style is best represented. Some of the finest work can be seen in the Minster and parish churches of York, but the style is found throughout the country. Apart from glass, surviving examples of monumental painting of the period *c.* 1390-1430 are rare, although *The Wilton Diptych* (Figure XIX) is evidence that work of the highest quality existed in panel painting.

Returning to miniature painting, it is quite likely that the illuminator of the French-influenced initials in *The Bedford Psalter and Hours* had encountered French manuscripts in England. The Duke of Bedford himself owned magnificent manuscripts decorated in France, and in the late 1430's and 1440's important patrons increasingly commissioned artists of French origin to illuminate their manuscripts. So lucrative was the English market for at least one French illuminator that he appears to have settled there. He was "The Fastolf Master," whose hand has been recognized in about eighteen manuscripts, some of which were executed for patrons in Normandy, and some for English patrons. Included in the latter category is *The Berkeley Hours* (New York, Pierpont Morgan Library, Ms. Glazier 9).

Figure XXII.
The Mirroure of The Worlde,
Oxford, Bodleian Library, Ms. Bodley 283.
Moses receiving the Ten
Commandments, fol. 1

In the face of this competition, English illuminators of the 1430's and 1440's
had little new to offer. The workshops of Scheerre and Johannes had evidently
broken up, but the International Style formulated by them continued in fashion.
This is demonstrated by a manuscript of *Select Psalms* executed *c.* 1440 for Humphrey, Duke of Gloucester (Figure XX). The only sign that the illuminator was
aware of developments outside England was his imitation in the borders of the
white vine ornament prevalent in Italian humanist manuscripts owned by the
Duke. A number of miniatures in a psalter and hours made between 1439 and 1446
for Henry Beauchamp, Earl of Warwick, are by an English artist still working
essentially in the tradition of Herman Scheerre (Plates 38, 39). It is exceptional, at
this period, that *The Warwick Psalter and Hours* was illuminated in England for an
important nobleman. Evidence suggests that English *limnours,* whose work was
less prized than that of their foreign colleagues, were increasingly forced to
decorate manuscripts in genres less prestigious than the devotional book: grants
of arms, charters, heraldic and genealogical manuscripts, and secular texts. This
change of emphasis is seen in the works of an artist, William Abell, who collaborated in *The Warwick Psalter and Hours.*

   Abell was probably the most important English illuminator working in the
middle years of the fifteenth century. In 1447-48 he was paid £1. 6s. 8d. for
decorating *The Consolidation Charter of Eton College.* Between 1452–53 and 1469–70
he was a citizen of London. At least seventeen illuminated manuscripts, in
addition to *The Warwick Psalter and Hours* and *The Eton College Consolidation Charter,*
have been attributed to him. These comprise five poems, three grants of arms and
charters, two statutes and ordinances, two rolls (one heraldic, the other religious),

Figure XXIII.
Writhe's Garter Book, Collection of
the Duke of Buccleuch and Queensberry
*A noble lady removing the stigma of
the white lace (part of the ceremony of
the Knighthood of the Bath), p. 128*

one book of hours, one missal, one cartulary, one astrological treatise and a Bible concordance.

Abell's early works, like *The Founder's Charter upon Act of Parliament for King's College, Cambridge,* dated 1446 (Figure XXI), retain much of the International Gothic style, with soft flowing draperies and faces delicately modeled with white highlights and touches of red. Already, however, the artist uses much harsher contrasts in color than had been common early in the century. This trend is more marked in his later manuscripts, such as *The Abingdon Missal* of 1461 (Plate 40), a work antithetical to the International Gothic style. Here the softly flowing draperies are replaced by sharp angular folds, and the figures are starkly outlined against the background by thick contour lines. Faces no longer have gentle, smiling expressions, and are vigorously modeled in red and pink.

Abell's work takes us into the 1460's. Thereafter, the decline in English manuscript illumination which had begun as far back as the 1430's and 1440's accelerates rapidly. Indigenous artists found it increasingly hard to compete with the superior Flemish manuscripts imported to meet the heavy demand for them among English patrons. At least one Netherlandish miniaturist was active in England *c.* 1470–90. This is the time span for a small group of works, including a copy of the Middle English *Mirroure of the Worlde* containing pen-drawings by a Flemish artist of considerable skill (Figure XXII).

Another heavy blow was dealt to English illumination with the introduction of printed books containing woodcut illustrations: William Caxton's first known work printed in England is dated 1476, and his first books containing woodcut illustrations were published in 1481. Some of the native illuminators produced

Map 1.
Map of England, showing the
principal centers of manuscript
production during the thirteenth to
fifteenth centuries.

books with borders imitating those in the "Ghent-Bruges" imported manuscripts. But to an even greater extent than in the middle years of the century, their output during the late fifteenth and early sixteenth centuries appears to have been largely confined to decorating heraldic and genealogical manuscripts. One example is *The Rous Roll,* made between 1483 and 1485 to commemorate the benefactors of Warwick and celebrate the deeds of the earls of Warwick. Two versions of the *Roll* exist, one in the College of Arms and the other in the British Library, Ms. Additional 48976. English artists also made pictorial records of important state ceremonials for precedence and reference. These were commissioned by the heralds, and in particular by John Writhe, Garter King of Arms from 1478 to 1504, and by his son and successor, Sir Thomas Wriothesley, Garter from 1505 to 1534. The Ceremony of the Knighthood of the Bath cycle, which forms part of a composite volume known as *Writhe's Garter Book,* was completed around 1488 and appears to have been made for John Writhe. With the exception of a single pen drawing by the Netherlandish artist mentioned above, the pictures are the work of two English painters, the better of whom is represented in Figure XXIII. *The Westminster Tournament Roll* of 1511 (London, College of Arms) and *The Parliamentary Procession Roll* of 1512 (Cambridge, Trinity College, Ms. 0.3.59), both executed for Thomas Wriothesley, are two of the largest works by English artists in the early sixteenth-century. The doll-like figures are not without a naïve, simple charm, and the frieze-like processions are of considerable decorative effect, but their chief value is historical and not artistic. The end had, to all intents and purposes, come fifty years earlier for the native English tradition of manuscript illumination.

LIST OF MANUSCRIPTS

THE LIFE OF SAINT CUTHBERT

London, British Library, Ms. Yates Thompson 26
135 x 98 mm.
Plates 1a and b, 2a and b

THE PSALTER OF ROBERT DE LINDESEY

London, Society of Antiquaries, Ms. 59
240 x 155 mm.
Plates 3, 4

A SINGLE LEAF FROM A PSALTER BY WILLIAM DE BRAILES

New York, Pierpont Morgan Library, Ms. M. 913
215 x 143 mm.
Plate 5

THE LIFE OF SAINT ALBAN

Dublin, Trinity College, Ms. E.I.40
240 x 165 mm.
Plates 6a and b, 7

THE MISSAL OF HENRY OF CHICHESTER

Manchester, John Rylands Library, Ms. lat. 24
305 x 196 mm.
Plates 8, 9

THE PARIS APOCALYPSE

Paris, Bibliothèque Nationale, Ms. Fr. 403
320 x 225 mm.
Plates 10, 11

THE TRINITY APOCALYPSE

Cambridge, Trinity College, Ms. R. 16.2
430 x 300 mm.
Plates 12, 13

THE OSCOTT PSALTER

London, British Library, Ms. Additional 50000
300 x 190 mm.
Plates 14, 15

THE RAMSEY PSALTER

New York, Pierpont Morgan Library, Ms. M. 302
St. Paul in Lavanttal, Stiftsbibliothek, Ms. XXV/2.
219
268 x 165 mm.
Plates 16, 17

THE TICKHILL PSALTER

New York, Public Library, Ms. Spencer 26
325 x 222 mm.
Plate 18

THE GORLESTON PSALTER

London, British Library, Ms. Additional 49622
374 x 235 mm.
Plates 19, 20

THE ST. OMER PSALTER

London, British Library, Ms. Yates Thompson 14
336 x 225 mm.
Plate 21

THE DE LISLE PSALTER

London, British Library, Ms. Arundel 83 pt. II
345 x 230 mm.
Plate 22

THE VIENNA BOHUN PSALTER

Vienna, Nationalbibliothek, Cod. 1826*
286 x 196 mm.
Plate 23

THE LIBER REGALIS

London, Westminster Abbey, Ms. 38
273 x 172 mm.
Plate 24

THE MISSAL OF ABBOT NICHOLAS LYTLINGTON

London, Westminster Abbey, Ms. 37
533 x 368 mm.
Plate 25

THE CARMELITE MISSAL

London, British Library, Mss. Additional 29704,
29705, 44892
787 x 560 mm.
Plates 26a and b, 27a and b

THE SHERBORNE MISSAL

Alnwick Castle, Collection of the Duke of Northumberland
533 x 380 mm.
Plates 28, 29, 30

THE BEAUFORT/BEAUCHAMP HOURS

London, British Library, Ms. Royal 2 A.XVIII
216 x 153 mm.
Plates 31, 32

THE PSALTER AND HOURS OF JOHN, DUKE OF BEDFORD

London, British Library, Ms. Additional 42131
407 x 279 mm.
Plates 33, 34a and b

'LI ROMANS DU BOIN ROI ALEXANDRE' AND MARCO POLO, 'LI LIVRES DU GRAUNT CAAM'

Oxford, Bodleian Library, Ms. Bodley 264
410 x 284 mm.
Plate 35

THE HOURS OF ELIZABETH THE QUEEN

London, British Library, Ms. Additional 50001
216 x 152 mm.
Plate 36

GEOFFREY CHAUCER: "TROILUS AND CRISEYDE"

Cambridge, Corpus Christi College, Ms. 61
315 x 222 mm.
Plate 37

THE PSALTER AND HOURS OF HENRY BEAUCHAMP, EARL OF WARWICK

New York, Pierpont Morgan Library, Ms. M. 893
273 x 186 mm.
Plates 38, 39

THE ABINGDON MISSAL

Oxford, Bodleian Library, Ms. Digby 227
358 x 242 mm.
Plate 40

SELECTED BIBLIOGRAPHY

The authors have chosen for the general bibliography works which contain a large selection of plates. In addition, some items discuss subject matter and patronage. Detailed bibliography of individual works is listed under the color plates and black-and-white figures.

GENERAL

Borenius, T., "The cycle of images in the palaces and castles of Henry III," *Journal of the Warburg and Courtauld Institutes,* VI (1943), pp. 40-50.

James, M.R., *The Apocalypse in Art,* London 1931.

Millar, E.G., *English Illuminated Manuscripts from the Xth to the XIIIth Century,* Paris 1926.

———, *English Illuminated Manuscripts of the XIVth and XVth Centuries,* Paris 1928.

Morgan, N., *Early Gothic Manuscripts 1190-1285. A Survey of Manuscripts illuminated in the British Isles.* 4. London 1980 (in the press).

Pächt, O., Alexander, J.J.G., *Illuminated Manuscripts in the Bodleian Library, Oxford. 3 British, Irish and Icelandic Schools,* Oxford 1973.

Rickert, Margaret, *Painting in Britain. The Middle Ages,* 2nd ed., Harmondsworth 1965.

Saunders, O.E., *English Illumination,* Paris 1928 (repr. New York 1969).

EXHIBITIONS

Medieval Art in East Anglia 1300-1520, Norwich, Castle Museum, 1973.

English Illuminated Manuscripts 700-1500, Brussels, Bibliothèque Royal Albert ler, 1973.

British Heraldry from its Origins to c. 1800, London, British Museum, 1978.

BIBLIOGRAPHY TO INDIVIDUAL MANUSCRIPTS

PLATES 1 & 2
Forbes-Leith, W., *The Life of St. Cuthbert,* Edinburgh 1888.

Baker, M., "Medieval illustrations of Bede's Life of St. Cuthbert," *Journal of the Warburg and Courtauld Institutes,* XLI (1978), pp. 16-49.

Morgan, N., *Early Gothic Manuscripts 1180-1285. A Survey of Manuscripts illuminated in the British Isles,* 4. London 1980 (in the press), No. 12.

PLATES 3 & 4
Haseloff, G., *Die Psalterillustration im 13 Jahrhundert,* Kiel 1938, pp. 14ff. Tab. 2.

Ker, N.R., *Medieval Manuscripts in British Libraries. I. London,* Oxford 1969, pp. 302-3.

Morgan, N., *op. cit.,* No. 47.

PLATE 5
"A newly discovered miniature by W. de Brailes," *Thirteenth Report to the Fellows of the Pierpont Morgan Library* (1963/4), 11-13.

Morgan, N., *op. cit.,* No. 72.

PLATES 6 & 7
Jacob, E.F., James, M.R., *Illustrations to the Life of St. Alban in Trinity College Dublin MS E.1.40,* Oxford 1924.

Henderson, G., "Studies in English Manuscript Illumination, I," *Journal of the Warburg and Courtauld Institutes,* XXX (1967), p. 73ff.

Harden, A.R., *La Vie de Seint Auban,* Anglo-Norman Text Society 19 (1968).

Morgan, N., *op. cit.,* No. 85.

PLATES 8 & 9
Legg, J. Wickham, *The Sarum Missal,* Oxford 1916.

James, M.R., *A descriptive catalogue of the Latin manuscripts in the John Rylands Library at Manchester,* Manchester 1921, pp. 73-75.

Hollaender, A., "The Sarum Illuminator and his school," *Wiltshire Archaeological and Natural History Magazine* 50 (1943), pp. 232-238.

Morgan, N., *op. Cit.,* No. 100.

PLATES 10 & 11
Delisle, L., Meyer, P., *L'Apocalypse en français au XIIIe siècle (Paris, Bibl. Nat. fr. 403),* Paris 1901.

Turner, D.H., "The Evesham Psalter," *Journal of the Warburg and Courtauld Institutes,* XXVII (1964), p. 31ff.

Henderson, G., "Studies in English Manuscript Illumination, II," *Journal of the Warburg and Courtauld Institutes,* XXX (1967), p. 104ff.

Morgan, N., *op. cit.,* No. 103.

PLATES 12 & 13
James, M.R., *The Trinity College Apocalypse,* Roxburghe Club 1909.

Brieger, P., *The Trinity College Apocalypse,* London 1967.

Henderson, G., "Studies in English Manuscript Illumination, II," *Journal of the Warburg and Courtauld Institutes,* XXX (1967), pp. 117ff.

———, "Studies in English Manuscript Illumination, III," *Journal of the Warburg and Courtauld Institutes,* XXXI (1968), pp. 108ff.

Otaka, Y., Fukui, H., *Apocalypse Anglo-Normande (Cambridge, Trinity College, MS R.16.2),* Centre de Recherches Anglo-Normandes, Osaka 1977.

Morgan, N., *op. cit.,* No. 110.

PLATES 14 & 15

Warner, G., *Descriptive catalogue of the manuscripts in the Library of C.W. Dyson Perrins*, Oxford 1920, pp. 40-47.

Haseloff, G., *op. cit.*, pp. 61ff. Tab. 16.

Turner, D.H., "Two rediscovered miniatures of the Oscott Psalter," *British Museum Quarterly*, XXXIV (1970), pp. 10-19.

Morgan, N., *op. cit.*, No. 151.

PLATES 16 & 17

Sandler, L.F., *The Peterborough Psalter in Brussels and other Fenland Manuscripts*, London 1974, pp. 39ff.

———, "Christian Hebraism and the Ramsey Abbey Psalter," *Journal of the Warburg and Courtauld Institutes*, XXXV (1972), pp. 123-134.

PLATE 18

Egbert, D.D., *The Tickhill Psalter and related manuscripts*, New York 1940.

Alexander, J.J.G., "English early fourteenth century illumination: recent acquisitions," *Bodleian Library Record*, IX (1974), pp. 76ff.

———, *The Decorated Letter*, New York 1978, pl. 31.

PLATES 19 & 20

Cockerell, S.C., *The Gorleston Psalter*, London 1907.

Thompson, E. Maunde, "The Gorleston Psalter," *Burlington Magazine*, 13 (1908), pp. 146-51.

Warner, G., *Descriptive catalogue of the Manuscripts in the Library of C.W. Dyson Perrins*, Oxford 1920, No. 13.

Pächt, O., "A Giottesque Episode in English Mediaeval Art," *Journal of the Warburg and Courtauld Institutes*, VI (1943), pp. 51, 53.

Medieval Art in East Anglia 1300-1520, Norwich, Castle Museum 1973, No. 20.

PLATE 21

Thompson, H. Yates, *Facsimiles in Photogravure of Six Pages from a Psalter, Written and Illuminated about 1325 A.D., for a Member of the St. Omer Family in Norfolk*, London 1900.

Weale, W.H.J., et al., *A Descriptive Catalogue of the Second Series of Fifty Manuscripts in the Collection of Henry Yates Thompson*, Cambridge 1902, No. 58.

Millar, E.G., *English Illuminated Manuscripts of the XIVth and XVth Centuries*, Paris 1928, pp. 8-9, 48-49, pls. 19, 20.

Pächt, O., "A Giottesque Episode . . .," *art. cit.*, pp. 52-53.

Medieval Art in East Anglia 1300-1520, *op. cit.*, No. 28.

PLATE 22

Sandler, L.F., "A follower of Jean Pucelle in England," *Art Bulletin*, 52 (1970), pp. 363-372.

———, "An early fourteenth century English Breviary at Longleat," *Journal of the Warburg and Courtauld Institutes*, XXXIX (1976), p. 11ff.

PLATE 23

James, M.R., Millar, E.G., *The Bohun Manuscripts*, Roxburghe Club 1936, pp. 33-46, pls. XXXIX-LVI.

Simpson, A., "The Connections between English and Bohemian Painting during the second half of the fourteenth century," unpublished doctoral thesis, University of London 1978, pp. 119-135.

PLATE 24

Beauchamp, Earl, *Liber Regalis*, Roxburghe Club 1870.

Simpson, A., *op. cit.*, pp. 147-153.

PLATE 25

Legg, J. Wickham, *Missale ad usum ecclesie Westmonasteriensis*, Henry Bradshaw Society, 3 vols., 1891-96.

Millar, E.G., *op. cit.*, pp. 28-29, 87, pls. 71, 72.

English Illuminated Manuscripts 700-1500, Brussels, Bibliothèque Royale Albert Ier, 1973, No. 71.

Simpson, A., *op. cit.*, pp. 137-142.

PLATES 26 & 27

Rickert, Margaret, *The Reconstructed Carmelite Missal*, London 1952.

PLATES 28-30

Thompson, E. Maunde, "Notes on the Illuminated Manuscripts in the Exhibition of English Medieval Painting," *Proceedings of the Society of Antiquaries of London*, 2nd ser. XVI (1895-97), pp. 226-230.

Legg, J. Wickham, "Liturgical Notes on the Sherborne Missal, a Manuscript in the Possession of the Duke of Northumberland at Alnwick Castle," *Transactions of the St. Paul's Ecclesiological Society*, IV (1896), pp. 1-32.

Herbert, J.A., *The Sherborne Missal*, Roxburghe Club 1920.

PLATES 31 & 32

Kuhn, C.L., "Herman Scheerre and English Illumination of the Early Fifteenth Century," *Art Bulletin*, 22 (1940), pp. 140ff.

Panofsky, E., *Early Netherlandish Painting*, Harvard 1953, pp. 116-118.

Rickert, Margaret, "The So-called Beaufort Hours and York Psalter," *Burlington Magazine*, 104 (1962), pp. 238-246.

Alexander, J.J.G., "William Abell 'lymnour' and 15th Century English Illumination," *Kunsthistorische Forschungen Otto Pächt zu seinem 70 Geburtstag*, Salzburg 1972, p. 166.

Turner, D.H., "The Wyndham Payne Crucifixion," *British Library Journal*, 2 (1976), pp. 16-21.

PLATES 33 & 34

Turner, D.H., "The Bedford Hours and Psalter," *Apollo*, 76 (1962), pp. 265-270.

———, "The Wyndham Payne Crucifixion," *art. cit.*, pp. 21-22.

PLATE 35

Millar, E.G., *op. cit.*, pp. 36, 87, pls. 86, 87.

James, M.R., *The Romance of Alexander MS. Bodley 264*, Oxford 1933.

Pächt O., Alexander, J.J.G., *Illuminated Manuscripts in the Bodleian Library, Oxford. 3 British, Irish and Icelandic Schools*, Oxford 1973, No. 793.

PLATE 36

Weale, W.H.J., *op. cit.*, No. 59.

Thompson, H. Yates, *Illustrations from One Hundred Manuscripts in the Library of Henry Yates Thompson*, vol. IV, London 1914, No. 59.

Millar, E.G., *op. cit.*, pp. 36, 89, pls. 88-90.

Turner, D.H., "The Bedford Hours and Psalter," *art. cit.*, p. 270.

——, "The Wyndham Payne Crucifixion," *art. cit.*, p. 12.

PLATE 37

Galway, M., "The Troilus Frontispiece," *Modern Language Review*, XLIV (1949), pp. 161-177.

Pearsall, D.A., "The Troilus Frontispiece and Chaucer's Audience," *Yearbook of English Studies*, VII (1977), pp. 68-74.

Parkes, M.B., Salter, E., *Geoffrey Chaucer, Troilus and Criseyde*, Cambridge 1978, pp. 15-23.

PLATES 38 & 39

Warner, G., *Descriptive Catalogue of Illuminated Manuscripts in the Library of C.W. Dyson Perrins*, Vol. 1, Oxford 1920, No. 18.

Alexander, J.J.G., "William Abell...," *art. cit.*, pp. 166, 168-169.

Mediaeval & Renaissance Manuscripts, New York, Pierpont Morgan Library 1974, No. 34.

PLATE 40

Millar, E.G., *op. cit.*, pp. 40, 77, 92, pl. 100.

Pächt, O., Alexander, J.J.G., *op. cit.*, No. 1065.

Alexander, J.J.G., "William Abell...," *art. cit.*, p. 168.

BIBLIOGRAPHY OF BLACK AND WHITE FIGURES.

Figure I

Warner, G.F., and Gilson, J.P., *Catalogue of Western Manuscripts in the Old Royal and King's Collections*, London 1921, I, pp. 36-38.

Morgan, N., *op. cit.*, No. 2.

Figure II

Pächt, O., Alexander, J. J. G. *Illuminated Manuscripts in the Bodleian Library, Oxford 3. British, Irish and Icelandic Schools*, Oxford 1973, No. 334.

Morgan, N., op. cit., No. 19.

Figure III

Cockerell, S.C., *W. de Brailes*, Roxburghe Club 1930.

Pollard, G., "William de Brailes," *Bodleian Library Record*, V (1955), p. 204.

Morgan, N., *op. cit.*, No. 72.

Figure IV

James, M.R., "The drawings of Matthew Paris," *Walpole Society*, XIV (1925/26), p. 18ff.

Vaughan, R., *Matthew Paris*. Cambridge 1958.

Morgan, N., *op. cit.*, No. 92.

Figure V

Haseloff, G. *op. cit.*, p. 61ff. Tab. 16.

Hollaender, A., "The Sarum Illuminator and his school," *Wiltshire Archaeological and Natural History Magazine*, 50 (1943), pp. 239-48.

Morgan, N., *op. cit.*, No. 101.

Figure VI

James, M.R., *La Estoire de Seint Aedward Le Rei*, Roxburghe Club 1920.

Henderson, G., "Studies in English Manuscript Illumination, I," *Journal of the Warburg and Courtauld Institutes*, XXX (1967), pp. 80ff.

Morgan, N., *op. cit.*, No. 123.

Figure VII

Warner G.F., Gilson, J.P., *Catalogue of Western Manuscripts in the Old Royal and King's Collections*, London 1921, I, p. 15.

Branner, R., "The Johannes Grusch Atelier and the Continental origins of the William of Devon painter," *Art Bulletin*, 54 (1972), pp. 24-30.

Bennett, A.L., "Additions to the William of Devon group," *Art Bulletin*, 54, tr (1972), pp. 31-40.

Morgan, N., *op. cit.*, No. 159.

Figure VIII

James, M.R., *The Apocalypse in Latin and French (Bodl. MS Douce 180)*, Roxburghe Club 1922.

Hassall, A.G., Hassall, W.O. *The Douce Apocalypse*, London 1961.

Henderson, G., "An Apocalypse Manuscript in Paris (Bibl. Nat. MS lat. 10474)," *Art Bulletin*, 52 (1970), pp. 22-31.

Morgan, N., *op. cit.*, No. 153.

Figure IX

Wormald, F., "Paintings in Westminster Abbey and contemporary paintings," *Proceedings of the British Academy*, XXXV (1949), pp. 161-76.

Tristram, E.W., *English Medieval Wall Painting, II, The Thirteenth Century*, Oxford 1950, passim.

Figure X

Cockerell S.C., James, M.R., *Two East Anglian Psalters at the Bodleian Library, Oxford. The*

Ormesby Psalter and the Bromholm Psalter, Roxburghe Club 1926.

Pächt, O., "A Giottesque Episode . . .," *art. cit.,* pp. 53-55.

Medieval Art in East Anglia, op. cit., No. 21.

Figure XI

Warner, G., *Queen Mary's Psalter,* London 1912.

Pickering, O.S., "Some similarities between Queen Mary's Psalter and the Northern Passion," *Journal of the Warburg and Courtauld Institutes* XXXV (1972), pp. 135-44.

Roberts, M., "Towards a literary source of the Passion in Queen Mary's Psalter," *Journal of the Warburg and Courtauld Institutes,* XXXVI (1973), pp. 361-365.

Alexander, J.J.G., "English early fourteenth century illumination . . .," *art. cit.,* pp. 72-74.

Figure XII

James, M.R., *The Treatise of Walter of Milemete,* Roxburghe Club 1913.

Figure XIII

Tristram, E.W., *English Wall Painting of the Fourteenth Century,* London 1955, pp. 48-58, 206-219, pls. 1-5, 6a and b.

Brown, R.A., Colvin, H.M., Taylor, A.J., *The History of the King's Works, II, The Middle Ages,* London 1963, pp. 518-519.

Rickert, M., *Painting in Britain. The Middle Ages,* 2nd ed. Harmondsworth 1965, pp. 150-151.

Van Geersdaele, P.C., Goldsworthy, L.J., "The Restoration of Wall-painting Fragments from St. Stephen's Chapel, Westminster," *The Conservator,* 2 (1978), pp. 9-12.

Figure XIV

Pächt, O., "A Giottesque Episode . . .," *art. cit.,* pp. 69-70.

⸻, Alexander, J.J.G., *op. cit.,* No. 653.

English Illuminated Manuscripts 700-1500, op. cit., No. 68.

Figure XV

Leroquais, V., *Les Psautiers manuscrits des bibliothèques publiques de France,* II, Mâcon 1940-41, pp. 45-46, pls. CV-CX.

Wormald, F., "The Fitzwarin Psalter and its Allies," *Journal of the Warburg and Courtauld Institutes,* VI (1943), pp. 71-79.

English Illuminated Manuscripts 700-1500, op. cit., No. 69.

Figure XVI

Reproductions from Illuminated Manuscripts, British Museum, Series II, London 1910, No. XVI.

Rickert, M., *Painting in Britain . . ., op. cit.,* p. 165.

Figure XVII

Vor Stefan Lochner Die Kölner Maler von 1300 bis 1430, Cologne, Wallraf-Richartz Museum, 1974, No. 84.

Spriggs, G.M., "The Nevill Hours and the School of Herman Scheerre," *Journal of the Warburg and Courtauld Institutes,* XXXVII (1974), pp. 104ff.

Turner, D.H., "The Wyndham Payne Crucifixion," *art. cit.,* 13-15.

Figure XVIII

James, M.R., "An English Medieval Sketchbook, No. 1916 in the Pepysian Library, Magdalene College, Cambridge," *The Walpole Society,* XIII (1924/25), pp. 1-17.

Wormald, F., "The Wilton Dipytch," *Journal of the Warburg and Courtauld Institutes,* XVII (1954), pp. 194-195.

Figure XIX

Wormald, F., "The Wilton Diptych," *art. cit.*

Harvey, J.H., "The Wilton Diptych — A Reexamination," *Archaeologia,* 98 (1961), pp. 1-28.

Figure XX

Alexander, J.J.G., "William Abell . . .," *art. cit.,* p. 169.

British Heraldry from its Origins to c. 1800, London, British Museum, 1978, No. 212.

Figure XXI

Alexander, J.J.G., "William Abell . . .," *art. cit.,* pp. 166-167.

English Illuminated Manuscripts 700-1500, op. cit., No. 82.

Figure XXII

Scott, K.L., "A mid-fifteenth-century English illuminating shop and its customers," *Journal of the Warburg and Courtauld Institutes,* XXXI (1968), pp. 170-196.

⸻, *The Caxton Master and his Patrons* (Cambridge Bibliographical Society Monograph No. 8), Cambridge 1976, pp. 25-46.

Figure XXIII

Wagner, A.R., *Heralds of England,* Oxford 1967, p. 138, pls. X-XII.

Scott, K.L., *The Caxton Master . . ., op. cit.,* pp. 47-54.

Backhouse, J., Review of Scott in *Medium Aevum,* XLVII (1978), pp. 202-205.

British Heraldry . . ., op. cit., No. 262, color plate.

ACKNOWLEDGEMENTS

The authors and publishers would like to express their sincere thanks to the following institutions and individuals who kindly provided materials and granted permission to reproduce them in this volume.

COLOR PLATES

ALNWICK CASTLE, By Courtesy of the Duke of Northumberland, Plates 28, 29, 30.

CAMBRIDGE, The Master and Fellows of Corpus Christi College, Cambridge University, Plate 37.

CAMBRIDGE, The Master and Fellows of Trinity College, Cambridge University, Plates 12, 13.

DUBLIN, The Board of Trinity College, Plates 6a, 6b, 7.

LONDON, Reproduced by Permission of the British Library Board, Plates 1a, 1b, 2a, 2b, 14, 15, 19, 20, 21, 22, 26a, 26b, 27a, 27b, 31, 32, 33, 34a, 34b, 36.

LONDON, Society of Antiquaries, Plates 3, 4.

LONDON, By Courtesy of the Dean and Chapter of Westminster, Plates 24, 25.

MANCHESTER, The John Rylands University Library, Plates 8, 9.

NEW YORK, The New York Public Library, Plate 18.

NEW YORK, The Pierpont Morgan Library, Plates 5, 16, 17, 38, 39.

OXFORD, The Bodleian Library, Plates 35, 40.

PARIS, The Bibliothèque Nationale, Plates 10, 11.

VIENNA, The National Library, Plate 23.

BLACK AND WHITE PLATES

CAMBRIDGE, The Syndics of Cambridge University Library, Figure VI.

CAMBRIDGE, Reproduced by Permission of the Syndics of the Fitzwilliam Museum, Cambridge, University, Figure III.

CAMBRIDGE, The Master and Fellows of King's College, Cambridge University, Figure XXI.

CAMBRIDGE, By Permission of the Master and Fellows, Magdalene College, Cambridge, Figure XVIII.

LONDON, Reproduced by Permission of the Trustees of the British Library Board, Figures V, VII, XI, XII, XVI, XVII, XX.

LONDON, Reproduced by Courtesy of the Trustees of the British Museum, Figure XIII.

LONDON, The Duke of Buccleuch and Queensbury, Figure XXIII.

LONDON, Reproduced by Courtesy of the Trustees, The National Gallery, London, Figure XIX.

LONDON, By Courtesy of the Dean and Chapter of Westminster, Figure IX.

OXFORD, The Warden and Fellows of All Souls College, Oxford, Figure IV.

OXFORD, The Bodleian Library, Figures II, VIII, X, XIV, XXII.

PARIS, Bibliothèque Nationale, Figure XV.

WINDSOR, The Provost and Fellows of Eton College, Figure XVIII.

PLATES AND COMMENTARIES

PLATE 1

THE LIFE OF SAINT CUTHBERT

London, British Library, Ms. Yates Thompson 26
135 x 98 mm.

*T*his small book contains *Bede's Life of Saint Cuthbert* and other texts relating to the saint. It belonged to the Cathedral Priory of Durham and is listed in the medieval library catalogues. The manuscript is believed to have been made in the scriptorium of the Priory because its text is closely related to the library's surviving unillustrated version. Its stylistic connections with several late twelfth-century manuscripts from this center (e.g., Oxford, Bodleian Library Ms. Douce 270) as well as parallels in style with the seal of Prior Bertram (1189–1212), still preserved in the Durham Cathedral Library, suggest that this version of the saint's life illustrated with forty-six miniatures was made *c*. 1200. The style is a painterly version of Durham and North English work of a few decades earlier: e.g., *The Bible of Hugh de Puiset* (Durham, Cathedral Library, Ms.A.II.1) and *The Gough Psalter* (Oxford, Bodleian Library, Ms. Gough lit. 2). There may also have been some knowledge of South English work, such as that of the late artists of *The Winchester Bible* (Winchester, Cathedral Library).

A. fol. 26   *Cuthbert sails to the land of the Picts*

The illustrations of Cuthbert's life are remarkable for the directness and simplicity of the presentation of narrative. Each scene is focussed upon the action of the saint himself without subsidiary figures distracting the eye from the central event of the story. This miniature shows Cuthbert on a sea journey with two companions to the lands of the Niduari, a tribe of the Picts. The boat on a "mound" of sea is set against an abstract background of a gold panel on a red ground, a compositional device that accents the narrative by isolating the group of figures as the focal point of the scene. The simplicity of the composition is enhanced by the plain gold frame.

B. fol. 35v   *Cuthbert teaching the monks of Lindisfarne*

After some years at Melrose Abbey in the Scottish Lowlands, Cuthbert was transferred to the monastery at Lindisfarne off the coast of Northumbria. This miniature shows him teaching the monks. Because this copy of his life was made for the monastery at Durham, the successors of the monks of Lindisfarne, the illustrations emphasize the monks' activities, sometimes slanting the narrative to call attention to a particular issue. The painterly style, modeled faces and rather squat figures with naturalness of draperies and pose, is well depicted in this scene. The gold ground has a punched pattern, a technique which became very popular later in the thirteenth century.

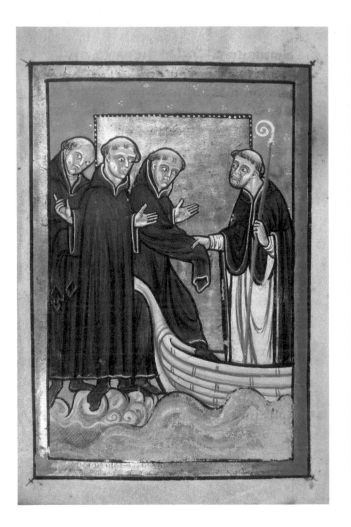

PLATE 2

THE LIFE OF SAINT CUTHBERT

London, British Library, Ms. Yates Thompson 26
135 x 98 mm.

A. fol. 71v   *Cuthbert takes a monk onto his boat as he retires to Farne Island*

*A*fter a period as a hermit on Farne Island Cuthbert was called back to an active life by his election as Bishop of Lindisfarne, but he eventually returned to Farne Island to end his days at his hermitage there. This miniature depicts Cuthbert, who holds his episcopal crozier and leaves his monks as one of them steps from the rocky shore into the boat. This monk's decision to accompany Cuthbert is emphasized by the saint's gesture of drawing him into the boat and his marked separation from the other monks by the prow of the boat. The gold panel in the background is an effective compositional device, as in Plate 1A.

B. fol. 74v   *The monks of Lindisfarne receive the signal from Farne Island of the news of Cuthbert's death*

This miniature is exceptional in that it attempts a landscape scene. A blue and green wavy sea separates Farne Island from Lindisfarne. Two laymen signal with torches the news of Cuthbert's death. One monk sitting on a rocky outcrop receives the signal while another moves off to carry the message to the monastery.

An earlier twelfth-century *Life of Saint Cuthbert* (Oxford, University College, Ms. 165) is illustrated with tinted drawings. A more elaborate version was made during the twelfth century but no longer survives. Whether this intermediary first introduced fully painted compositions or whether it was the artist of the copy we are considering is uncertain. The scenes were closely copied in monumental form during the late fifteenth-century, on the painted choir stalls of Carlisle Cathedral.

PLATE 3

THE PSALTER OF ROBERT DE LINDESEY

London, Society of Antiquaries, Ms. 59
240 x 155 mm.

fol. 35v   *The Crucifixion*

The ownership of Robert de Lindesey, Abbot of Peterborough (1214-22) is inscribed on the psalter on fol. iii. He is recorded as having owned two psalters, one with a commentary and one without; the latter is very probably the psalter illustrated here. The intended Peterborough destination is confirmed by the liturgical calendar, the litany, and the division of some of the psalms according to Benedictine use. There are three full-page illuminations, *The Crucifixion, Christ in Majesty,* and a large ornamental B for the first psalm. In addition there are three pages of tinted drawings of scenes from the Life of Christ. The production of the manuscript must antedate the death of Robert de Lindesey in 1222. In view of the dating of a stylistically similar psalter also intended for Peterborough Abbey (Cambridge, Fitzwilliam Museum, Ms. 12) after 1220, the Society of Antiquaries Psalter can perhaps be dated *c.* 1220-22.

The group of Christ, the Virgin and St. John in this miniature of the Crucifixion is below the personifications of the Sun and the Moon. Roundels at the upper corners of the frame show female figures representing the Church, holding the Chalice, and the Synagogue, dejected with a broken staff, holds the Tablets of the Law of Moses. At the bottom, St. Peter and Moses represent the New and the Old Law, as a parallel to the two upper figures; at the sides are figures of prophets who had foretold the destiny of Christ.

The delicate body of Christ has a pitiful thinness, the more enhanced by contrast with the substantial figures of the Virgin and St. John. These two both sway away from the Cross with gestures of distress. St. Peter, Moses and the prophets in the frame all seem involved in contemplation of the Cross. The composition achieves its intimacy of grouping by focussing on the torso and head of Christ. The Cross is not of plain wood but is a "Living Cross" from which sprigs of foliage sprout. The idea conveyed is that the wood of the Cross is a symbolic Tree of Life through the redemption from sin and promise of resurrection given to man by the sacrifice of Christ. This imagery is used in hymns on the Cross, most particularly of the liturgy of Good Friday during the Adoration of the Cross.

The burnished gold ground against which the scene is set, and in the borders of the frame, has delicate incised patterns—an elaboration of the technique seen in Plate 1B.

PLATE 4

The Psalter of Robert de Lindesey

London, Society of Antiquaries, Ms. 59
240 x 155 mm.

fol. 36   *Christ in Majesty*

Christ is seated on a green arc within a mandorla, blessing with His right hand and holding an open book in His left. The symbols of the four Evangelists are in the corners of the frame and at midpoint of each side are busts of a woman and a man in half roundels. The delicate pose of the Christ is enhanced by the small head and the very tiny hands and feet, conveying an intimate impression. Christ does not appear as the terrifying judge of many twelfth-century paintings, but rather as beneficent and sympathetic. The relationship of the size of the figure to the frame is an important element of the style. The size and bulk of the figure is played down in contrast to late twelfth-century works like *The Westminster Psalter* (Figure I).

The small-scale delicate effect is enhanced by the detailed diaper pattern on the burnished gold. The modeling of the face and the relatively natural folds link the artist with the style of the early years of the century. His origins were perhaps in a style similar to that of *The Life of Saint Cuthbert.*

PLATE 5

A Single Leaf from a Psalter by William de Brailes

New York, Pierpont Morgan Library, Ms. M. 913
215 x 143 mm.

Scenes from the Infancy of Christ: the Magi come before Herod and his Advisers; Adoration of the Magi; Massacre of the Innocents; Flight into Egypt

This recently discovered single leaf by the Oxford illuminator William de Brailes forms a group with six similar leaves in the Fitzwilliam Museum, Cambridge, Ms. 330. One of the leaves depicts both *The Tree of Jesse* and the beginning of Psalm 1, suggesting that these miniatures were part of a series prefatory to a psalter. The set evidently had scenes from both Old and New Testaments, *The Last Judgment* and a *Wheel of Fortune*. In *The Last Judgment* a small tonsured figure is seen with a scroll inscribed *W. de Brail' me fecit*. A William de Brailes occurs in Oxford records of manuscript makers *c.* 1230-60, and there seems little doubt that he is the same person as *W. de Brail*. Several books are stylistically similar to the single leaves, suggesting that de Brailes was part of a large workshop, of which he was perhaps the head. The relative chronology of the workshop is difficult to determine as none of the works has any evidence of a firm date. The single leaves are perhaps *c.* 1230-40.

The page is divided into medallions in the manner of a stained glass window of the period, and this medium may well have influenced the arrangement. In the corners of the frame and at the sides are standing figures of the prophets who had foretold the coming of Christ. Animals and birds, purely decorative, fill the areas between the medallions containing the scenes of Christ's childhood.

The figures are rather wooden, but this effect is counteracted by liveliness of glance and gesture. The characters have an alertness of reaction which conveys a lively narrative. The highly burnished gold grounds have an incised diaper pattern which adds to the intricacy of the system of medallions. The same method of composition is seen in the Old Testament scenes in one of the Fitzwilliam Museum leaves. Small-scale figure-scenes and intricate decoration break up the page in the Early Gothic style: England was moving away from the monumentality and design clarity of the years around 1200. The stylistic origins of the artist can be found in *The Huntingfield Psalter* (New York, Pierpont Morgan Library, Ms. M. 43) and *The Lothian Bible* (New York, Pierpont Morgan Library, Ms. M. 791) which were probably made in Oxford between 1210 and 1220.

PLATE 6

THE LIFE OF SAINT ALBAN
Dublin, Trinity College, Ms. E.I.40
240 x 165 mm.

*T*his fully illustrated copy of *The Life of Saint Alban* incorporates scenes from the story of Saint Amphibalus, the priest who was saved by Alban's sacrificing himself as a substitute to the soldiers persecuting the Christians. There are also scenes of the visit of Saints Germanus and Lupus to England, and of the discovery and translation of the relics of Saint Alban. The main text is in the handwriting of the St. Albans monk and chronicler, Matthew Paris. Because the tinted drawings illustrating the text are in the style of the marginal drawings in the chronicles written in Matthew's own hand, there seems little doubt that he was the artist of all fifty-four illustrations in *The Life of Saint Alban*. The style of the drawing suggests that Matthew Paris executed this manuscript at the same time as the early parts of his chronicles (*c.* 1240–51) although the difference in size between the small marginal illustrations of the chronicles and the mostly half-page pictures of *The Life* make exact comparison difficult. An inscription on fol. 3 records the ownership of the book by St. Albans Abbey.

A. fol. 38   *The Martyrdom of Saint Alban*

This plate shows how the drawings are placed in relation to the text, occupying almost half the page above two columns of text, with titles set above the illustration. Two groups of men, some in chain mail and some holding spears, stand watching the beheading of Alban. The executioner became blind after beheading the saint, shown by his eyes falling from their sockets. A small dove representing Alban's soul flies upward. His severed head hangs on a tree, and the cross he has been holding is taken by a follower.

The drawing is given substance by the use of light color washes. The rounded contours of the figures and their lively facial expressions are characteristic of Matthew Paris's style. The height of the frame is taken up by the figures and the tree, producing a compressed effect typical of his composition.

B. fol. 45   *The Martyrdom of Saint Amphibalus*

The Governor of Verulamium (the Roman name of the present city of St. Albans) and a group of figures watch the slow martyrdom of Saint Amphibalus. The chief torturer has a winged cap, a feature often found on evil persons. He holds a bunch of rods for flagellation and plunges a dagger into the head of the saint. Two other men on the right puncture his body with spears and a dagger. An incision having been made in the saint's stomach, his entrails have been pulled out and wound around a stake. Amphibalus holds the same cross which Alban had held at his martyrdom.

The lively but rather naïve facial expressions, with the figures completely filling the frame are similar to those in Plate 6A.

i decole mi glutz de palm dauban du brant acerin. Huit cumence au sarrazin du marcur clarte sanz fin.
Lun tent vert ciel lautre en declin du vespre lun laut au matin. Un cstien ki ueisin la cir hut tcinte en sae rosin

17

l raenel as sanc du blanc hi cur finut.   Il est mic de sun faic lunccl chorc

ente ac tuier tur tanut at un heure la blelce au merctr. A une cltache en terre fiche atache.
qel h fuint enuurimer. E la entraille fi elculer. He lesta par ceu ciuet suftir. P serimm paent oltir.

amphibal.

29

C ucrou le pendirent li giu desloial   A mphibal amu deu ki tut ad a guier
A i dist amphibal uest pas cist cinent tal   H us ucum ta la gloire ke ds uus ueut dun

aracle

18

Pur nuf prier celui kest uerai messiaz   E Auban ki chief est ia du bu coupe.
Ki en croiz mor suffri thu ia par iudaf   Va quere tun seinnur tun maist e auoue
Kil tuit ki sa feiture sumef ne uendre pas   Sun chief nummat mui e un astre luc

PLATE 7

The Life of Saint Alban

Dublin, Trinity College, Ms. E.I.40
240 x 165 mm.

fol. 38v.   *Heraclius is mocked for taking down Alban's head from the tree*

*H*eraclius, one of the men involved in the execution of Alban, had been so overwhelmed by the courage and faith of the saint that he resolved to become a Christian. The Governor and his men mock Heraclius for taking Alban's head down from the tree. Subsequently, he too suffered martyrdom by beheading.

The use of tinting to model the figures is particularly evident in the Governor and the man standing in front of the horse. The round contours and flowing curves of Matthew Paris's compositions are also clear. His head types nearly always are wide-eyed, and rounded faces predominate. This individual style is quite distinct from two other illustrated Lives of the Saints with tinted drawings which have been linked to "The School of St. Albans":*Life of Saint Thomas* (Private Collection); *Life of Saint Edward the Confessor* (Cambridge, University Library, Ms. Ee. 3. 59). They may derive from original versions designed by Matthew Paris but they differ in many points of composition from his work.

PLATE 8

THE MISSAL OF HENRY OF CHICHESTER

Manchester, John Rylands Library, Ms. lat. 24
305 x 196 mm.

fol. 150   *Henry of Chichester kneeling before the Virgin and Child*

The donor in this scene of the Virgin and Child, a tonsured cleric, is probably the Henry of Chichester whose ownership is implied by a late thirteenth-century note on fol. 1. He was Precentor (an ecclesiastical functionary) of Crediton in Devon, and is recorded in a 1277 inventory of Exeter Cathedral for the donation of a missal which is described in the 1327 catalogue of the library as having gilded pictures. The connection with other manuscripts from the Salisbury region (the group of "the Sarum Master" who is so-called from the Roman name of Salisbury, the city in which he worked) and the accurate Salisbury text of the missal make it very likely that the book was produced there. Although later in the thirteenth century, and in the fourteenth and fifteenth centuries, the liturgical "Use of Salisbury" was adopted by almost all the dioceses of Southern England, it is exceptional to find accurate texts outside the Salisbury diocese *c.* 1250. There are eight full-page miniatures and twelve historiated initials, a luxurious program of decoration unusual for the text of a missal. The occurrence of the feast of St. Edmund of Abingdon in the original hand in the Calendar means the book must postdate his canonization in 1246.

During the thirteenth century the physical and emotional relationships in a devotional image between the donor figure and the Virgin, Christ, or a saint, become increasingly close. This picture is one of the most advanced examples from the middle years of the century. Henry of Chichester in alb and cope kneels before the Virgin and Child, holding a scroll *Fili Dei miserere mei* (O Son of God have mercy upon me). The Child with one hand on His Mother's collar, leans down to take with His other hand the scroll, while both He and His Mother are gazing down at the priest. Above, two angels swing censers about the Virgin and Child just as an image within the church where Henry served would have been censed. It is almost as if Henry of Chichester were kneeling before such a statue which suddenly came alive to answer his petition. At the foot of the throne the presence of three lion cubs makes a subtle comment: the medieval book of animal lore, the Bestiary, relates that lion cubs are born as if dead, but on the third day after birth their father breathes on them and they come alive. Similarly, the Christ Child on His Mother's lap is to be the Christ who will be raised from the dead after three days: Henry of Chichester's plea for mercy would appear to be addressed both to the Child and to the resurrected Christ who will be his Judge.

The style is characterized by elongated figures, by delicate rather small heads, and by an emphasis on linear folds within the context of a painterly style. This artist's work indicates a liking for monumental dramatic compositions, suggesting origins in a large-scale medium, such as wall-painting.

PLATE 9

THE MISSAL OF HENRY OF CHICHESTER

Manchester, John Rylands Library, Ms. lat. 24
305 x 196 mm.

fol. 152v   *The Resurrection*

Christ steps out of the tomb holding the cross pennant of victory over death, while the soldiers sleep below. The inclusion of two angel musicians vigorously playing beside Christ is almost unique. The figure of Christ well demonstrates the style of "the Sarum Master." He is elongated and thin with the flesh areas lightly modeled. The two angels have the white hatching which characterizes this artist's creation of highlights. In several instances the figures overlap the edges of the frame, appearing to pull the composition forward. Some evidence indicates that "the Sarum Master" derived his style and some features of his subject matter from painting around 1200, which he reinterpreted more elegantly. The face of Christ is a gentler Gothic version of the Byzantine-derived heads of the period of *The Westminster Psalter* (Figure I). The monumental aspects of his figures have more in common with that period than with his immediate predecessors (e.g. Plates 3-5).

PLATE 10

THE PARIS APOCALYPSE
Paris, Bibliothèque Nationale, Ms. Fr. 403
320 x 225 mm.

fol. 2   *St. John before Domitian; St. John in the cauldron of boiling oil*

*T*his apocalypse, which has a French text and is illustrated with tinted drawings, has often been ascribed to "the School of St. Albans." Its style is,
however, quite distinct from that of Matthew Paris, being much closer to the work
of "the Sarum Master," particularly *The Amesbury Psalter* (Figure V); it is very
probably by his hand. There is no evidence of its medieval ownership or of its
date, but comparison with the works of "the Sarum Master" suggests that it is
c. 1245-55.

Some of the illustrated copies of the Apocalypse have a series of scenes of the
Life of St. John, the author of the book, whose visions are so dramatically
described in the text. These form a separate section before and after the text, as a
set of full-page pictures. Here John is brought before the Emperor Domitian and
condemned to be placed in a cauldron of boiling oil outside the Latin Gate in
Rome. The saint was completely unharmed by the boiling oil, which is also being
poured over his head by one his tormentors. His naked figure with hands raised in
prayer is being led away on the right after his torture has ended.

Although the tinted-drawing technique is quite different from his normal fully
painted illumination, the artist probably is "the Sarum Master" (Plates 8, 9, Figure
V). A restricted range of light color washes is applied to the edges of the folds and
occasionally over all the drapery. The drawing is characterized by elaborate
systems of troughed folds and complicated fussy edges on draperies. These
features contrast with Matthew Paris's work although he uses the same technique, also the less crowded and compressed composition, allowing more space
above the heads of the figures.

PLATE 11

THE PARIS APOCALYPSE
Paris, Bibliothèque Nationale, Ms. Fr. 403
320 x 225 mm.

fol. 44 v   *St. John drinks from the poisoned cup; his last mass and death*

St. John was challenged by a priest of the Temple of Diana to drink from a poisoned cup as proof of the power of his God. The pagan falling to the ground is dying from the poison, whereas John, protected by the hand of God, is unharmed. The scene below shows John praying at the altar at his last mass. A tomb by the altar was supposed to have been prepared for him into which he stepped and lay down to die. He is in the tomb in his mass vestments and his soul is being carried up to heaven by angels. These final scenes of the Life of St. John are placed after the Apocalypse illustrations. Some similar scenes of his life are found in two slightly later Apocalypses (New York, Pierpont Morgan Library, Ms. M.524, Oxford, Bodleian Library, Ms. Auct. D.4.17) that are also closely related in their series of Apocalypse illustrations. Although these three manuscripts are linked in subject matter they are distinctly different in style, and are by three artists whose only stylistic connection is the use of tinted drawing.

PLATE 12

THE TRINITY APOCALYPSE

Cambridge, Trinity College, Ms. R. 16.2
430 x 300 mm.

fol. 15   *The calling down of fire from Heaven and the worship of the statue of the Beast*

This is the most lavish of all the English thirteenth-century Apocalypses, having mostly fully painted miniatures with much use of burnished gold. The text is a French translation from the Latin with a French commentary. It is the work of several artists whose styles on the one hand have links with the drawing of Matthew Paris, the art of "The Sarum Master," and on the other with the new French-influenced manner which appears in *The Life of Saint Edward the Confessor* (Figure VI). Ownership by a lady of the court circle, possibly Queen Eleanor herself, has been suggested in view of the presence of aristocratic ladies in several of the miniatures, and the inclusion of figures of friars, who at the time were much favored by the court circle. This evidence is, however, very weak and no definite conclusion can be made regarding the possible owner. The presence of the new French-influenced style in some of the miniatures assigns it to the decade 1250-60 when this new manner first appears.

Chapter XIII vv. 11-15 of the Apocalypse is here represented: "And I beheld another beast coming up out of the earth; and he had two horns like a lamb, and he spake as a dragon. And he exerciseth all the power of the first beast before him, and causeth the earth and them which dwell therein to worship the beast whose deadly wound was healed. And he doeth great wonders so that he maketh fire come down from heaven in the sight of men. . . . And he had power to give life to the image of the beast, that the image of the beast should both speak and cause that as many as would not worship the image of the beast should be killed."

The Apocalypse is fully painted with the scenes set against blue and red panels on the ground. In contrast with most other Apocalypses of the period, the miniatures are set at various positions in the text rather than at the head of each page. Such an archaic arrangement, combined with the earlier compositional device of a panel in the ground (see Plates 1, 2), suggests that *The Trinity Apocalypse* may have depended upon an earlier thirteenth-century model, but as the extant Apocalypses are all post-1240, there is really no proof that such a system of illustration existed earlier. The artist may have chosen an archaic feature deliberately.

The figure style in this plate has links with both "the Sarum Master" and with Matthew Paris; its forms and draperies are closer to the former, and the facial types to the latter. Several artists worked on the Apocalypse in slightly varying versions of the style.

pas escrit en le liuere de uie del aignel ki est ostis de
la nesaunce del munde. Ki ad ozilles oid. Ki ad ame
ne en cheitiuisun. il irrat en cheitiuisun. e ki tuez scie
espee. il li kouent estre ostis de espee. Ceist est la patien
ce e la fei des seinz.

P la reste ke e une nenie ostis mes ansi tum ostis. est en
tendu blasfemie. la quele mes ke ole seit en pensee de
akeuns maueis. il ne la osent demustrer. Mes li diable
resuscitera ceste reste en auntcrist. Il aorunt auntcrist.

ceul ki sur signifiez p tere. e le diable en lu disaunz
nul ne estre semblable a lu. Il fra baraile od les sem
blanz disaunt akeuns. uns autres en espauntaunt.
e au derin en turmentaunt ke il les amene en sa errur.
E si il por estre ke les eslus seient mene en errur. Il les
ueintera ne mi en surmuntaunt mes en truuaunt. Le
liuere de uie est la pdestinaciun de deu en quele pdesti
naciun les reprouez ne sunt pas escrit. Li aignel est dit
ostis del comencement del munde pur co ke sa mort est
pfigure en le pmerein homme. e en abel. e in ysaac. e iosep.

C lo ui une autre beste muntaunt de la tere. e il
auer deus corns semblable al aignel. e il parla
si cum le dragun. e il feseit tute la pouste de la beste
deuaunt sun esgard. e il fist la tere. e tuz le habitauz
en lu aorer la premereine beste. de ki la plaie de mort
est garie. e il fist graunt signes. adecertes issi ke il feist
fu decendre del cel en tere. en le esgard des houmes.

C este beste signifie un des deciples auntcrist plus
maueis des autres. u uns ki le precherunt. La que
le uindra de la tere. co est de la cumpanie as reprouez.
P les deus corns poi entendre les giue e les paens ke il de
ceueta. kar li diable ki parole p auntcrist. il plora p
sas deciples. Il fra tute la pouste de la pmereine beste en
le esgard de lu. co signifie en nun de lu. Auntcrist e sas de

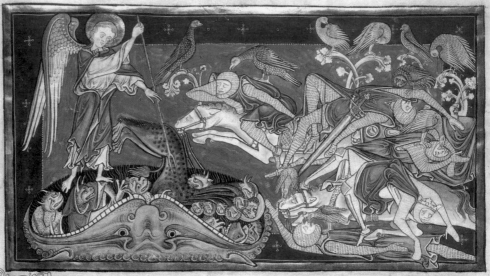

 E la beste est prise e od lu le faus pphete ki tult sig
nes deuaunt lu. p les queus il traï ceus ki res
ceurent le mark de la best. e ki aozerent le ymagine de lu
i tel deu sur mis uiss en le estaunk de fu ardaunt de
sufre. e les autres sunt ostus en le espeie del seaunt sur le
cheual. ki isseit de sa buche. e tus les oiseaus sunt asa
ulés de lur chars.

La beste serra pse e le faus pphete de lu. kaunt cele
chose serra pempli. ke li apostle seint poul dist. E nostre
seignur ihu tuwera. p le espirit de sa buche. e destrui
ra p la uisitaciun de sa uenue. Aunterist e li faus pphe

fut mis uiss en le estaunk de fu. c'est cus mis en lur
malice durrant en lu treske a la fin de lur uie.
Co ke il dist ke les autres sunt ostu en le espeie del se
aunt sur le cheual. c'este raweisun il mist pur con
fusiun. kar les seinz le eprise de queus est entendu p
la espie. gaberunt les desleaus kaunt aunterist serra
tuwe. pur coke il qdeterunt le tresreual houme e le plus
mauueis de tute gent estre deu nent mortel. ki il sa
ueient estre tuwe p resmauueise mort. Les oiseaus ser
rut asaulés de lur chars. pur coke tuz les eluz se cloi
rrut mut. de lam ort aunterist. pur co ke la misericorde
de deu lur ad deliuere de si tresmauuel enemi.

Le put de abisme.

Io ui un aungele detendaunt del cel auaunt la
clef de abisme. e une graunt cheene en sa main.
e il prist le dragun le auncien serpent ki est le diable
e satanas: e le lia p mil auns. e le mist en abisme eil

c'est aungele signefie crist. Sun detendre del cel:
est sa incarnaciun. Il ad la clef de abisme c'o
est de enfer. pur coke il gare ceus ke il uoit de la en
trete. e il soefre ceus ke il uoit cheir dreitureaument

PLATE 13

The Trinity Apocalypse

Cambridge, Trinity College, Ms. R. 16.2
430 x 300 mm.

fol. 23 v   *The Battle against the Beast: his defeat and imprisonment*

*T*hese miniatures illustrate Chapter XIX vv. 20-21 and Chapter XX vv. 1-3: "And the beast was taken, and with him the false prophet that wrought miracles before him, with which he deceived them that had received the mark of the beast, and them that worshipped his image. These both were cast into a lake of fire burning with brimstone. And the remnant were slain with the sword of him that sat upon the horse, which sword proceeded out of his mouth: and all the fowls were filled with their flesh. And I saw an angel come down from heaven having the key of the bottomless pit and a great chain in his hand. And he laid hold on the dragon, that old serpent, which is the Devil and Satan, and bound him for a thousand years, and cast him into the bottomless pit and shut him up . . ."

The first miniature depicts the casting into the lake of fire, represented as the Mouth of Hell in the form of the gaping jaws of an animal. The fowls of the air are feeding on the followers of the beast. The three events of the imprisonment of the dragon are combined in the lower miniature. As in Plate 12, St. John is standing beside his vision. Although the expression on his face hardly changes from scene to scene in this Apocalypse, in later examples he reacts psychologically to the dramatic events which take place before him.

PLATE 14

THE OSCOTT PSALTER

London, British Library, Ms. Additional 50000
300 x 190 mm.

fol. 9v   *The Adoration and Dream of the Magi*

*T*his richly decorated psalter has twenty-two full-page miniatures prefatory to the text of the Psalms. Ten pages are devoted to the Life of Christ and ten to the figures of the Apostles. A missing leaf which was recently discovered (now London, British Library, Ms. Additional 54215) has a picture of a bishop who may be the intended owner. The presence of rare Italian saints in the Calendar, together with unusual aspects of the Bishop's vestments have given rise to the supposition that he may be Ottobuono Fieschi, the Papal legate to England from 1265 to 1268. Although plausible, this supposition lacks strong proof. The Calendar also reveals a particular interest in St. Modwenna of Polesworth (Warwicks.) and it is difficult to understand why the Papal legate, if he was the owner, should have had a devotion to her. The Psalter came from St. Mary's College, Oscott, near Birmingham, by whom it was owned in the nineteenth century and from whom it has taken its name.

The format of roundels for the scenes, two to a page, is unusual in England. In this miniature of *The Adoration and Dream of the Magi* subsidiary medallions have censing angels at the top, the horses of the Magi at the bottom, and *the Creation of Adam* and *the Creation of Eve* in the middle of the sides. The burnished gold grounds have a punched design of circles and dots. It is difficult to see the relevance of the Old Testament subjects to the New Testament events depicted.

The very individual style of the artist is partly influenced by French sources as shown by the angular broad folds of the draperies, a style which had come into French painting c. 1250, also a tendency to over-large heads, some of very severe expression, and a preference for angular poses. The colors are dominated by a brilliant deep blue, a bright orange-red, and the burnished gold, colors typical of contemporary French illumination.

The style has been generally considered as that of the English "Court School" as represented by *The Douce Apocalypse* (Figure VIII), but the scenes in *The Oscott Psalter* lack the refinement of the Apocalypse and of the earlier products of "the Court School" such as *The Life of Saint Edward the Confessor* (Figure VI). The compositions have narrative vigor without the restrained elegance of the court works. The asymmetry of the side medallions is unusual, suggesting an original source in a system having four large roundels within a single frame, or, alternatively, a compositional device reminiscent of a diptych with the larger side medallions on the outer edges. Between the Gospel scenes are full-page illuminations of the standing Apostles, also apparently meant to be seen in pairs as in diptychs. Unfortunately the leaves of this section of *The Oscott Psalter* have been misbound making it difficult to assess fully the intended compositional arrangement.

PLATE 15

THE OSCOTT PSALTER

London, British Library, Ms. Additional 50000
300 x 190 mm.

fol. 16v   *The Betrayal; Christ before Pilate*

The two scenes in the main roundels are accompanied by subsidiary medallions of angels at the top, two male heads, probably advisers of Pilate, at the bottom, and *the Offerings of Cain and Abel* and *the Murder of Abel* at the sides. These Old Testament scenes refer to the Sacrifice of Christ in his Passion, because Abel who offers a Lamb and is killed by Cain is a parallel to Christ.

Both New Testament scenes have individual features of composition. In *the Betrayal* the circular frame forces the evil leering heads of those arresting Christ inwards towards him, thus intensifying the drama. In the bottom scene Pilate's vigorous gesture and pose, and the sly expression and attitude of the adviser leaning over his shoulder, contrast with the calmness of Christ.

The angular broad triangular folds derived from contemporary French painting are clearly evident in the figure of Christ, although other aspects of the style are unrelated to France.

PLATE 16

THE RAMSEY PSALTER

New York, Pierpont Morgan Library, Ms. M. 302
St. Paul in Lavanttal, Stiftsbibliothek, Ms. XXV/2.
19
268 x 165 mm.

fol. 3v   *Noli me tangere; Doubting of Thomas; Ascension; Pentecost*

This psalter, which has a calendar of the Benedictine Abbey of Ramsey, has been divided. Most of the prefatory full-page miniatures are in the Pierpont Morgan Library in New York; the main psalter text is in the Abbey of St. Paul in Lavanttal, Austria. An added portrait medallion at the foot of the calendar page for December shows William of Grafham who was cellarer of Ramsey during the abbacy of John of Sawtry (1286-1316). The main artist, who painted the full-page miniatures, also worked on a psalter for Peterborough Abbey (Brussels, Bibliothèque Royale, Ms. 9961-62) made between 1299 and 1317. *The Ramsey Psalter* seems earlier and may even have been made shortly before 1300.

The eleven prefatory miniatures of this psalter have Old and New Testament scenes and events from the Lives of the Saints, mostly with four scenes to a page, as in this example. They are characterized by rather squat figures with gentle facial expressions, lively gestures and a sinuous relaxed sway; standing figures have a dance-like manner, well illustrated by the figure of Christ in the *Noli me tangere*. Within the groups a rhythm of composition is conveyed by complementary swaying poses and gestures of the hands, as in *The Doubting of Thomas, Ascension* and *Pentecost* scenes. This style, in contrast to the angular elements evident in *The Oscott Psalter* (Plates 14, 15), depicts the more relaxed manner in the last quarter of the thirteenth century. The use of the ogee arch to frame the scenes is well suited to the curving poses of the figures. The alternating colors of the frame, the backgrounds, and the area behind the ogee arches, are a rhythmic counterpoint to the whole page. The overall fussiness in patterns of color and ornament is a counterpart in painting to the aesthetic of the Decorated Style in English architecture and sculpture of the period.

PLATE 17

THE RAMSEY PSALTER

New York, Pierpont Morgan Library, Ms. M. 302
St. Paul in Lavanttal, Stiftsbibliothek, Ms. XXV/2.
19
268 x 165 mm.

fol. 4   *The Death, Assumption and Coronation of the Virgin*

*I*n order to give the impression that *the Coronation* is taking place in Heaven and that in *the Assumption* the Virgin is carried up to Heaven, the artist has departed from the usual format of four scenes to a page, reading from top to bottom. Here the narrative starts at the lower left with the Virgin's death and continues on the lower right as the Virgin in a mandorla is raised out of the frame into Heaven by angels where *the Coronation* takes place in the upper register. Beneath a wide ogee arch Christ blesses the crowned Virgin, while above them, a pair of angels swing censers. On the left under a pointed arch stands Saint John the Evangelist, and on the right under another isolating arch, Saint John the Baptist. *The Coronation,* the main scene, is set against a gold ground with an incised diaper pattern, the only unit of the composition given this background. The squat proportions of the figures are clearly evident in the two saints in the upper panel, as are the characteristic rhythmic effects of pose, drapery, decorative pattern and color.

PLATE 18

THE TICKHILL PSALTER

New York, Public Library, Ms. Spencer 26
325 x 222 mm.

fol. 51   *Psalm 52. Scenes of the Life of David from II Samuel, Chapter II, vv. 1-7*

This is one of the most elaborately decorated psalters of the thirteenth and fourteenth centuries, with illuminated borders and marginal scenes intended for every page, and particularly rich decoration at the liturgical divisions of the psalms. Such a vast program of decoration was not completed in the last section of the text and the illuminations have been left at various stages of development. A fifteenth-century inscription on the first folio records that the book was written and gilded by John Tickhill, Prior of the monastery of Augustinian Canons at Worksop (1303-1313). The Litany seems intended for Worksop, so this later inscription may be correct in its attribution: Worksop is in Nottinghamshire which was in the diocese of York. Manuscripts related stylistically to *The Tickhill Psalter* are associated with this region and the artists' workshops may have been in the Midlands or the North.

Almost all illuminated psalters have large historiated initials at the first psalms sung daily at Matins and at the first psalm for Sunday Vespers. *The Tickhill Psalter* is exceptionally elaborate at these divisions, having as the historiated initial for *Psalm 52* almost a full-page illumination, with the first words of the psalm in gold capitals as a single line below. The D of the large initial is repeated in the small gold capital. The subject is unusual. It is part of the very large cycle of the Life of David which is extended over the initials and the lower margins of almost all the psalter. The two upper scenes in the initial consist of the Lord instructing David to go to Hebron in Judah. Below, David with his wives Ahinoam and Abigail come to Hebron, and on the right David is anointed as King of Judah. In the lower margin David is told that the men of Jabesh-gilead were those that had buried Saul, and in the second scene David is sending messengers to the men of Jabesh-gilead. The texts intended for the scrolls held by the figures have not been inscribed, but the trailing scrolls themselves form an integral part of the overall design. In the fourteenth century heraldic decoration is frequent in manuscript illumination, some directly related to ownership, but much of it purely ornamental. The five shields on the *Psalm 52* page bearing the arms of England and France, and of the Hastings, Clare and Percy families, seem to have no significance for intended ownership.

The figure style is more like contemporary French work than that of *The Ramsey Psalter* (Plates 16,17), which is more characteristically English. The figures in *The Tickhill Psalter* are slightly elongated and the compositions calm and elegant. The punched patterns on the gold and the ornament are part of an English tradition. Since the late-thirteenth-century, border decoration had become increasingly elaborate, the borders acting as a platform and frame for marginal illustrations. These illustrations are sometimes narrative episodes as the two here, or more usually "grotesque" subjects with animals and hybrid figures like the half-man half-animal blowing a trumpet at the bottom left. These grotesques often grow out of, or form part of, the structure of the border itself. Curving foliage sprays are used to balance the composition of the whole page. As in *The Ramsey Psalter* a complex decorative system of ornament and figures combine to form an overall pattern.

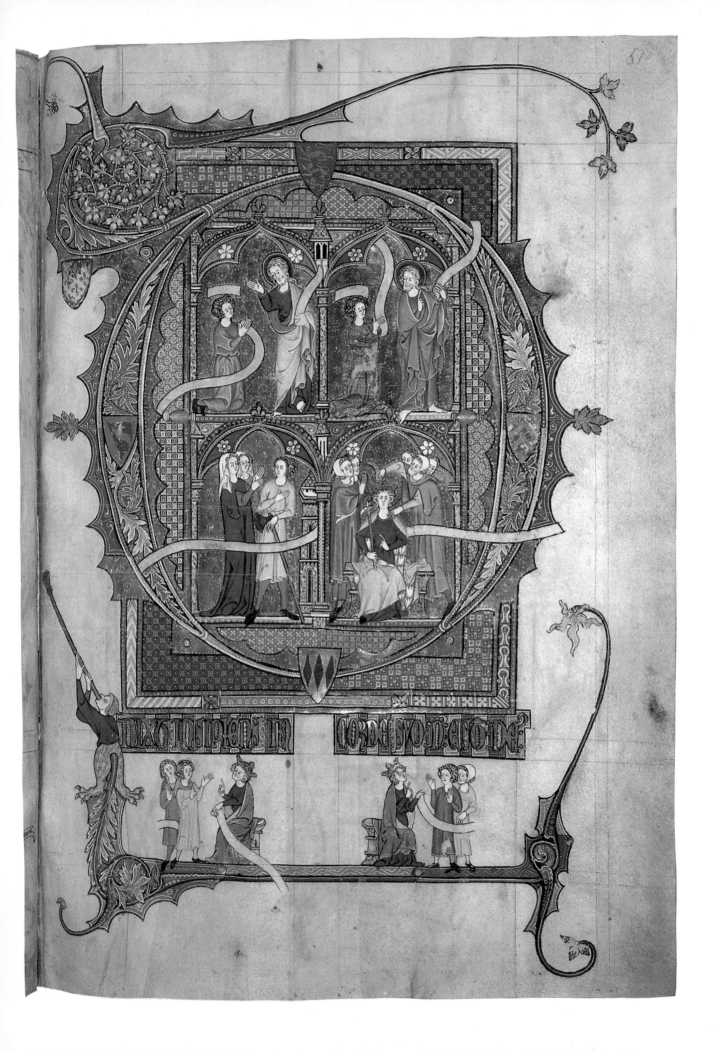

Dixit insipiens in corde suo non est deus

PLATE 19

THE GORLESTON PSALTER
London, British Library, Ms. Additional 49622
374 x 235 mm.

fol. 8 *Psalm 1. Tree of Jesse; Annunciation; Visitation; Nativity; Adoration; Presentation*

The calendar of this psalter has on the 8th March the Feast of the Dedication of the Church of Gorleston in Norfolk. Several pages have border illuminations of donors kneeling before St. Andrew, the patron saint of Gorleston church. One of these figures bears the arms of Roger le Bigod, Earl of Norfolk (*d.* 1306). He is accompanied by a Benedictine monk who might be Thomas le Bigod, who became prior of the Cluniac Priory of Thetford in 1304. The main decoration of the psalter might date from as early as 1304, but slightly later in the second decade is more likely. Richly illuminated borders with marginal grotesques are on almost every page. *The Crucifixion* page is in an Italianate style which must have been added later, *c.* 1320-30, and may have been painted when the book passed to Norwich Cathedral Priory; its ownership is attested to by an added Litany of their use. *The Ormesby Psalter* (Oxford, Bodleian Library, Ms. Douce 366) has added illuminations by the same artist, and was given to the Cathedral Priory in the early 1320's by the monk Robert Ormesby.

Psalm 1, the first psalm of Sunday Matins, is given the richest decoration of all the liturgical divisions of the text. The initial B is filled with *the Tree of Jesse* showing the ancestry of Christ from the sleeping Jesse. The frequent choice of this subject for this initial is perhaps because verse 3 of the psalm refers to a tree which brings forth fruit. Around the B is a heraldic border of the arms of England and France. The upper three sides of the border are filled with seated kings and prophets, an extension of *the Tree of Jesse* theme. In the lower border are scenes of *the Annunciation, Visitation, Nativity, Adoration of the Magi* and *Presentation in the Temple.* At the bottom in the margin is *David's defeat of Goliath,* probably alluding to the last verse of the psalm which says that the "ungodly shall perish." The hunting of the stag above the lower border is frequently shown on the page for *Psalm 1.* The stag is a symbol of the soul that is attacked by the huntsmen who are "the ungodly" and thus the scene makes a general allusion to the text of the psalm.

The figure style shows complex mannered poses with cascades of voluminous folds having prominent highlights on their edges. The faces have stereotyped expressions of surprise. A similar figure style is found in *The Howard Psalter* (London, British Library, Ms. Arundel 83 pt. I) which can be perhaps dated *c.* 1309-26. The crowding together of figures and foliage in a complex decorative system is a feature comparable to *The Tickhill Psalter* (Plate 18), but bears no connection in style and ornamental type.

non abuit in confilio impiorum
& in uia peccatorum non ftetit: &
in cathedra peftilentie non fedit.
Sed in lege dñi uoluntas eius:
& in lege eius meditabitur die ac nocte.

PLATE 20

THE GORLESTON PSALTER

London, British Library, Ms. Additional 49622
374 x 235 mm.

fol. 7   *The Crucifixion*

*T*en or more years after the decoration of the main part of the psalter was completed, this single painting of *the Crucifixion* was added. The long body of Christ hangs heavily on the cross, the Virgin and St. John clasp their hands in expressions of grief, and St. Mary Magdalen kneeling at the foot of the cross gazes up at the figure of Christ. A three dimensional rocky ledge represents Golgotha, the place of the skulls, as indicated by skulls and bones on the ground. The gold background is punched with a very intricate diaper pattern; the frame has medallions of the Evangelist symbols in the corners, Saints Paul and Peter at the sides, a crowned female saint at the top and a male saint at the bottom. Between these medallions in the border bars are the alternating arms of England and France.

The significance of this *Crucifixion* is its strong dependence on an Italian model —either Sienese, or from a center influenced by Sienese painting. The rocky ledge and the pose of St. Mary Magdalen occur in Crucifixions by Simone Martini. The weight of Christ's body is completely in the Italian style, contrasting with the lighter, tauter Christs of contemporary English work. Modeling and highlighting of draperies, bodies and faces is achieved with little use of line, whereas English painting of the period is dominated by linear effects. The small slit-eyed faces seem to be the English artist's interpretation of Italian heads, as is the fuzzy hair best seen in the medallion in the center of the bottom frame. Despite the strong Italian element the poses and draperies of the Virgin and St. John are distinctly English. In general, although Italian influence occurs frequently in English fourteenth-century painting from this time on, it is almost always assimilated into English traditions of style, composition and subject matter.

A single full-page *Crucifixion* is unusual for a psalter; the subject as a single miniature usually decorates a missal (e.g. Plate 25), and it is possible that this painting derives from an example in a missal.

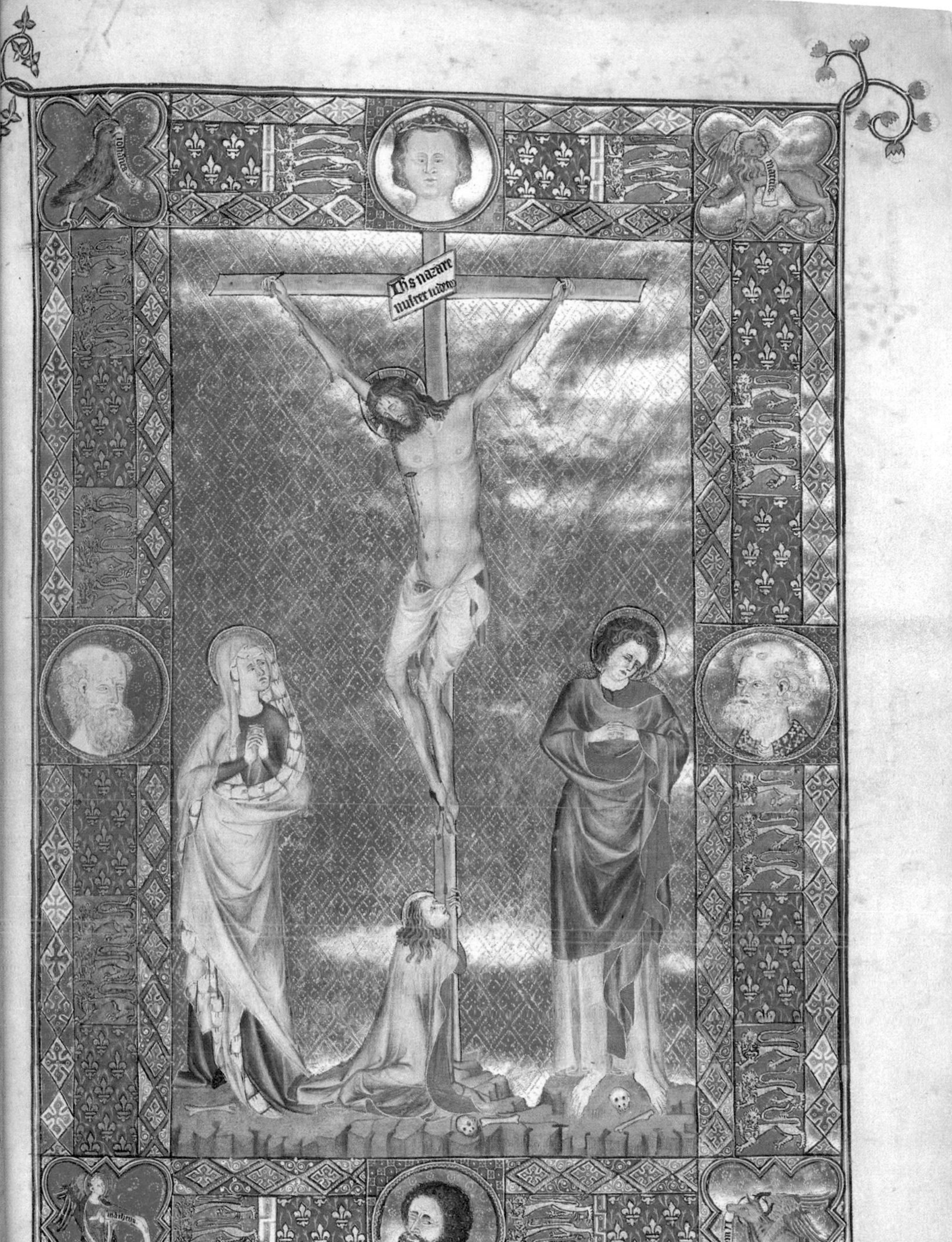
Ihs nazare
nus rex iudeo

PLATE 21

THE ST. OMER PSALTER

London, British Library, Ms. Yates Thompson 14
336 x 225 mm.

fol. 120   *Psalm 109. The Last Judgement*

*T*he St. Omer Psalter, begun 1330-40, is one of the last masterpieces of East Anglian illumination. It was commissioned by a knight of the St. Omer family of Mulbarton, near Norwich, who is depicted on fol. 7 kneeling with his wife. The decoration was not completed until 1414-22, when the volume came into the possession of Humphrey, Duke of Gloucester. His erased inscription of ownership is on fol. 173.

The original illumination includes full borders and large historiated initials to the main psalm divisions on fols. 7, 57v, 70v and 120. Within the initial to the psalm *Dixit dominus* is *the Last Judgement*, a subject not often found in English psalters of the first half of the fourteenth century. Christ is seated in judgment, showing His wounds and flanked by angels summoning the dead from their tombs. The graves are represented in receding rows, giving an impression of spatial depth beyond the surface of the page. The dead themselves—clergy and laity of all ranks—rise in various poses. A head emerges in the first row; in the center a figure is levering himself out on his elbows; on the right a pair of legs appears out of a grave. Two more dead emerge outside and below the frame of the initial. The corresponding angels at the top hold emblems of Christ's Passion, the theme also of the nine roundels in the border: commencing in the lower left border the scenes represent *the Betrayal, the Flagellation, the Carrying of the Cross, the Crucifixion, the Entombment, the Resurrection, the Three Marys at the Sepulchre, the Ascension* and *Pentecost.*

The design of the page and the figure style are characteristic of the last phase of East Anglian illumination. The profuse foliate ornamentation of the borders (which include two wrestlers at the top) is typical of the manuscripts of this region. The figures, silhouetted dramatically against the gold-tooled grounds, are heavily modeled with orange-brown flesh tints. This three-dimensional treatment, and the accomplished rendering of spatial depth in the main initial, reveal the influence of Italian early Trecento painting. The group of artists who executed the added *Crucifixion* page (fol. 7) in *The Gorleston Psalter* (Plate 20) and the *The Douai Psalter* (Douai, Bibliothèque Municipale Ms. 171) are responsible for the decoration of this page.

xit dns do
mino me
o: sede a
dextris me
is. Donec
ponam in
imicos tu
os: scabel
lum pedum tuorum.

irgam uirtutis tue emittet dns ex sy
on: dominare in medio inimicorum tuorum.

ecum principium in die uirtutis tue in spl[e]
doribus sctor: ex utero ante luciferum genui te.

irauit dns et non penitebit eum: tu es
sacerdos in eternum.secm ordine melchisedech.

ominus a dextris tuus: confregit in di
e ire sue reges.

udicabit in nacionibz implebit ruinas:

PLATE 22

THE DE LISLE PSALTER

London, British Library, Ms. Arundel 83 pt. II
345 x 230 mm.

fol. 134v   *The Coronation of the Virgin*

This psalter is the second part of a composite volume. The first part, folios 1–116, known as *The Howard Psalter*, was made either for Sir William Howard of East Winch, Norfolk (*d*. 1308), or John Fitton of Wiggenhall, Norfolk (*d*. 1326) An inscription dated 1591 on folio 3, records that the manuscript was in the possession of Lord Howard of Naworth. *The De Lisle Psalter*, folios 117–135, takes its name from the inscription recording the gift of the book in 1339 by Robert de Lisle to his daughter Audere. It consists of a calendar and twenty-four full-page miniatures, including unusual theological diagrams. Two artists worked on the miniatures in the de Lisle section and there may have been some time lapse between the two sets of pictures. The first artist was apparently influenced by English work of 1320-30, if not earlier. The later artist, whose work is illustrated here, bears traces of French art of the workshop of the Parisian illuminator, Jean Pucelle. This second painter is called "The Majesty Master" after his painting of *Christ in Majesty* (fol. 130).

The larger-scale illumination of *the Coronation* appears almost to be a panel painting wherein Christ is shown placing the crown on the Virgin's head. Although two angel musicians are playing above, the composition is entirely dominated by the main figures and in this is markedly different from the same scene in *The Ramsey Psalter* (Plate 17). The monumentality of the figures is enhanced by contrast with the detailed diaper pattern of the background. The flowing curves of the draperies, the way in which they are modeled, the faces and poses, all are closely related to the Parisian art of Jean Pucelle and his workshop. The best similar examples are seen in such work of the 1330's as *The Prayer Book of Bonne of Luxembourg* (New York, Cloisters Museum), although its style does not have the monumental quality of *The De Lisle Psalter* miniatures. The French parallels and the inscribed date of the gift of the book place it between 1330 and 1339.

The very French style is in the same tradition as the slightly earlier *Queen Mary Psalter* workshop (Figure XI) and is markedly unlike the Italianate styles of some contemporary English artists (Plates 20, 21). Some of the stained glass at Wells Cathedral and York Minster is in the manner of *The De Lisle Psalter* artist, who may have derived the monumental aspect of his style from similar work in this medium or from panel painting.

antate do
mino can
ticum no
uum: quia
mirabilia
fecit.

Salua
uit sibi dex
tera eius: et
brachium

sanctum eius.

Notum fecit dominus salutare suum: in con
spectu gentium reuelauit iusticiam suam.

Recordatus est misericordie sue: et ueritatis
sue domui israel.

Uiderunt omnes termini terre salutare dei
nostri: iubilate deo omnis terra cantate et exulta
te et psallite.

Psallite domino in cithara in cithara et uo
ce psalmi: in tubis ductilibus et uoce tube cornee.

Iubilate in conspectu regis domini: moue
atur mare et plenitudo eius orbis terrarum et qui ha

PLATE 23

THE VIENNA BOHUN PSALTER

Vienna, Nationalbibliothek, Cod. 1826*
286 x 196 mm.
fol. 85v   *Psalm 97. The Crossing of the Red Sea*

*T*his volume is perhaps the earliest of the group of manuscripts made for the Bohun family. The erased name *Humfridus* which occurs three times (with various spellings) in some of the Collects (fols. 151v, 152v, 153), and the presence of the Bohun arms, establish that the book was written either for Humphrey de Bohun, Earl of Hereford from 1336, or his nephew, also named Humphrey, who succeeded him in 1361 and died in 1373. The former is more likely, as the arms of his sisters' husbands, James Butler, Earl of Ormond, and Hugh Courtenay, Earl of Devon, are found on fol. 7. A *terminus post quem* of 1340 is given by the arms of England quartering France ancient on the same folio.

The decoration of fols. 7-50v is still in the East Anglian tradition of the *St. Omer Psalter* (Plate 21) and thus points to a date between 1340 and 1361. The illumination from fol. 51 onward as well as the calendar on fols. 1-6v is quite different. Three hands can be distinguished in these folios of the manuscript. That their decoration was completed after 1374 is confirmed by the presence on fol. 141 of the arms of Thomas of Woodstock, Duke of Gloucester, the youngest son of Edward III. In that year he married Eleanor, daughter of the Humphrey de Bohun who died in 1373. Thomas was executed in 1397 and Eleanor died in 1399. Although her will mentions four psalters, the present volume cannot be identified as one of them.

The illumination of this manuscript follows the conventional formula for English Gothic psalters, with large historiated initials marking the main psalm divisions, in addition to many smaller initials and borders. The subject of the main initials is, however, most unusual. The scene depicted for *Psalm 97* is *the Crossing of the Red Sea,* or strictly speaking its immediate aftermath (Exodus, Chapter XV). The Israelites, having crossed the Red Sea, are in several groups. Moses, identifiable by his horns, is on the right, pointing with a rod to the waters, painted red, containing the bodies of drowned Egyptians. The animated group of men to the left is fashionably dressed in the costumes of the late fourteenth-century, complete with gold garters. The women of Israel are represented in the third group, also dressed in contemporary fashion; they are led by Miriam, playing a timbrel as in the Bible text. Some of the figures are singing the Song of Moses, praising the Lord for their miraculous deliverance. The words of the Song are close to those of *Psalm 97,* making the depiction of this Old Testament episode a suitable one for this psalm. The figures in the border roundels, praising the Lord with musical instruments, relate to verses 6 and 7 of the psalm. The roundels and the border decoration with its spiky leaves and grotesques indicate that the artist was steeped in the East Anglian tradition of the first half of the century. As with the illuminator of *The St. Omer Psalter,* he creates an illusion of spatial depth by placing the groups of Israelites in the initial on different levels of the rocky ground. This figure style has affinities with Flemish manuscripts. There is little modeling of faces, but draperies have delicate white highlights. The figures are sharply defined by thick lines, making them stand out against the gold-tooled ground.

PLATE 24

THE LIBER REGALIS

London, Westminster Abbey, Ms. 38
273 x 172 mm.
fol. 20   *The Coronation of a King and a Queen*

A group of English and French manuscripts exists, containing illustrated texts of coronation ceremonies and dating from the second half of the fourteenth century. Three are English: one is *The Lytlington Missal* (Plate 25), the second is in the Archivo General de Navarra, Pamplona, Spain, and the third is *The Liber Regalis*. Nothing is known of the origin of this last manuscript, but the glosses and marginal notes bring the text into concordance with the coronation ceremony of *The Lytlington Missal,* and show that it antedates 1383-84. If it was written for a specific coronation ceremony it would have been either that of Richard II which took place on July 16, 1377, or that of Anne of Bohemia who married Richard on January 22, 1382. The style of the illumination suggests that the latter date is more likely.

The text contains special rubrics (directions for procedure, so called because they were originally written in red) applicable to Westminster Abbey, but the manuscript is not mentioned in any of the Abbey inventories, because it was probably kept with the royal regalia. A note in the Abbey Muniments states that it was "in the Chapter Clerk's Custody June 21st 1762 and was placed in ye Record-room under the care of the Librarian in 1764."

The Liber Regalis contains four illustrations of coronation ceremonies, two full-page and two three-quarter-page. Illustrated here is the second, immediately preceding the text for the crowning of a king and queen. The couple, who may be intended to represent Richard II and Anne of Bohemia, are seated on two thrones, the queen's slightly lower than the king's. Four prelates are grouped behind the thrones, with another tier of four figures in livery very near the upper frame, the outer pair holding staves, the inner pair bearing crowns. All of the figures in this miniature are unnaturally tall and very slender, with heavily modeled, rather ugly faces, and strongly shaded draperies. Spatial depth is inconsistent: figures are piled up one above the other with no diminution in size towards the rear. Their animated gestures and close grouping give an atmosphere of liveliness and movement. The use of burnished gold for the back-drop, copes, crowns and outer frames creates a rich impression entirely appropriate to the theme of coronation, the most lavish and ostentatious of all state ceremonies.

The Liber Regalis has traditionally been considered to have been decorated by an artist brought over by Anne of Bohemia from her native land, or by someone strongly influenced by the style current in Prague. Bohemian influences are not evident, however, either in the border decoration which is English, or in the figure style which does not resemble that of contemporary Bohemian painting.

PLATE 25

THE MISSAL OF ABBOT NICHOLAS LYTLINGTON

London, Westminster Abbey, Ms. 37
533 x 368 mm.
Volume II, fol. 157v   *The Crucifixion*

*T*his Missal, which includes a text for royal coronations and funerals on fols. 206-224, was commissioned and given to Westminster Abbey by Nicholas Lytlington, Abbot between 1362 and 1386; his arms and initials occur on fols. 9, 21, 123, 157v, 225v, 263, 277v, 286v and 289. The date of the manuscript is precisely established by entries in the roll of the Abbot's Treasurer for 1383-84, which record payments for board and lodging of the scribe, Thomas Preston, and for materials, illumination and binding. These include 10 shillings paid *p(ro) pictur(a) dict(i) missal(is)*, presumably referring to *the Crucifixion* page; the total cost of the manuscript, now bound in two volumes, was £34. 14s. 7d. The missal is mentioned in a 1388 inventory of the Abbey vestry.

Two main artists illuminated the work with more than fifty historiated initials and small miniatures in addition to *the Crucifixion* page. The iconography of this *Crucifixion* is derived from Italian early Trecento painting and shows Christ and the two thieves surrounded by a crowd. The angels flying around Christ symbolize the sacramental nature of His sacrifice by catching in chalices the blood dripping from His wounds. To the left, below Christ, the centurion Longinus has just withdrawn the spear from Christ's side and is pointing to his own eye, a reference to an apocryphal legend in which the eye disease from which he suffered was cured by the flow of Christ's blood from the wound. The foreshortened figure of Stephaton on the other side of the Cross is proffering the sponge dipped in vinegar. On the extreme left the Virgin swoons into the arms of St. John, accompanied by her sister Mary Cleophas, and Mary Magdalen. The corresponding group on the right comprises three Jewish officials; the scrolls issuing from them bear texts from Matthew XXVII, verses 40 and 54.

The panels in the surrounding frame, separated by elaborate strapwork, illustrate other events of the Passion, commencing at the lower left with *the Betrayal* and followed clockwise by *Christ before Pilate, the Flagellation, the Carrying of the Cross, the Nailing to the Cross, the Deposition, the Entombment,* and *the Resurrection.* In the center of the upper frame the pelican pecking at her breast to feed her young symbolizes Christ's sacrifice. The shield of arms and initials in the lower frame are those of Abbot Nicholas Lytlington. The symbols of the four Evangelists are in quatrefoils at the corners of the frame.

Similarity to *The Liber Regalis* (Plate 24) may be seen in the buds coiling from the corners of the frame, but the figure style is quite different. The eyes of the larger figures have marked irises and pupils, and their highly set arched eyebrows and heavy lids often convey an expression of mingled surprise and solemnity.

The small *Crucifixion* in the lower margin had the practical function of protecting the full-page miniature from the ritual kisses of the priest at mass.

PLATE 26

THE CARMELITE MISSAL

London, British Library, Mss. Additional 29704, 29705, 44892
787 x 560 mm.

During the early years of the nineteenth century this volume was cut up and nearly 1600 fragments, consisting of initials, borders and some text, were mounted into scrapbooks. The original sequence was reconstructed by Margaret Rickert, who established that the missal was executed for an English Carmelite house, almost certainly that of the Whitefriars, London. The text appears to have been completed in or before 1393, but the illumination may have taken a few years longer. There are fifty-two miniatures which Miss Rickert attributes to no fewer than six different artists working in three basic styles. The four initials illustrated in this and the following plate are in these three styles.

A. fol. 193v   *Initial B introducing the Introit of the Votive Mass of the Trinity*

This initial is in the style of the Bohun group of manuscripts (Miss Rickert's Style C). The form of *the Holy Trinity*, combining with it the theme of *Christ in Judgement*, is typical of the fourteenth century. The latter is suggested by God the Father and Christ seated on a rainbow, by the Evangelists' symbols at the corners, and by the depiction of Christ displaying His wounds. The judgement theme is emphasized further by the presence of the Virgin in a form akin to that of the Woman of the Apocalypse "clothed with the sun, and upon her head a crown of twelve stars" (Revelations XII v. 1). The Virgin is also patroness of the Carmelite Order, shown by the texts she is holding, which are paraphrases of a versicle and an antiphon used in the Carmelite liturgy. In the initial the Virgin is acting as intercessor between the Holy Trinity and the kneeling man and woman, who may be the donors of the manuscript; they are flanked by their patron saints (St. Catherine of Alexandria is on the left).

B. fol. 38   *Initial C introducing the Introit of the Mass for Corpus Christi*

The Carmelite element is also prominent in this initial, which is in Miss Rickert's Style B and has strong affinities with *The Liber Regalis*. The celebration of mass in the lower half includes two Carmelite servers (the one on the left holds the elevation candle). The representation of *The Last Supper* and Christ's words on the scrolls instituting the Holy Sacrament appear to refer to the public refutation of Wycliffe's heretical views on transubstantiation on Corpus Christi Day, 1382, by a Carmelite named Peter Stokes. Wycliffe referred bitterly to Stokes as "a white dog," alluding to the color of the Carmelite habit. The two white dogs at the right appear to be a reference to this.

PLATE 27

The Carmelite Missal

London, British Library, Mss. Additional 29704, 29705, 44892
787 x 560 mm.

A. fol. 68v   *Initial T introducing the Introit of the Mass for the Dedication of a Church*

*T*hese two initials are in Miss Rickert's Style A, the most advanced of the three styles in the missal and apparently originating in the Low Countries. Fol. 68v shows the procession which circled the church three times during the dedication ceremony, led by three acolytes, one of whom is holding a processional cross. This group is followed by two choristers, a cleric bearing the bishop's crozier, the bishop, and finally five laymen, two of whom hold rosaries. The bishop is about to sprinkle holy water on the church in order to drive out the devil who is on the roof preparing to fly away. The shaft of the initial T is filled with blue angels, and it is supported by two figures. The splendid dromedary-like beast carrying the gold column and figure seems to be purely decorative.

B. fol. 93   *Initial S introducing the Introit of the Mass of the Purification of the Virgin*

The Purification takes place in an open chapel with a porch and a domed tabernacle over the protagonists: the Virgin holding out the Christ Child to the high priest Simeon. The chapel is diagonally in front of the initial S, with the porch on the left slightly nearer the spectator than is the right edge of the building. The receding tiled floor, the depiction of the vaults within the structure and the grouping of the figures in front of and behind the altar bear witness to the artist's command of perspective. The three-dimensional element is further emphasized by the modeling of faces and the sculptural treatment of drapery.

PLATE 28

The Sherborne Missal

Alnwick Castle, Collection of the Duke of Northumberland
533 x 380 mm.

p. 216   *The Mass for Easter Day*

This sumptuously illustrated volume was made for the Benedictine Abbey of Sherborne (Dorset). The joint patrons were Richard Mitford, Bishop of Salisbury (1396-1407), and Robert Bruyning, Abbot of Sherborne (1385-1415). A more precise dating for the decoration is suggested by the arms of Henry V as Prince of Wales on p. 81. He was given this title in 1400, and the ancient form of the French arms is used, which was altered officially to France modern around 1406.

The patrons are seen together on several pages, with Abbot Bruyning depicted alone nearly one hundred times. The scribe, a Benedictine monk named John Whas, and the illuminator, John Siferwas, also appear on various pages.

Not all the illumination is by Siferwas alone, although he was responsible for the entire decorative scheme. Most of the *Temporale* (pp. 13-358) is probably his work, as well as the full-page *Crucifixion* (p. 380). The calendar (pp. 1-12) and the *Ordo* and *Canon Missae*, the *Sanctorale, Commune Sanctorum* and the *Votive Masses* (pp. 359-689) were executed with the aid of one or more assistants.

That the decoration and iconography in this manuscript are highly individual, reflecting both the roles of the patrons and the personal taste of the artist, John Siferwas, is well demonstrated by the page shown here. The elaborate three-storied tabernacle contains *Noli me tangere, Christ in Majesty,* and, in the lowest section, the joint patrons, Bishop Mitford and Abbot Bruyning. Peter and Paul are among the four figures outside the tabernacle who flank Christ and the patrons. At the base kneel the scribe, John Whas, and the illuminator, John Siferwas, clad in the habits of a Benedictine monk and a Dominican friar respectively. The main initial contains *the Resurrection;* its precursors, or "types," *Samson carrying the Gates of Gaza, Jonah delivered from the Whale* and *the Lion breathing life into its Young* (see Plate 8) are found in the borders, accompanied by three more Old Testament scenes which are the counterparts of *the Harrowing of Hell.* This elaborate typology conforms to a long tradition in English miniature and monumental painting stretching back to the twelfth century. The remaining border and marginal decorations, the "portrait" heads, the *vignettes* in the lower border of knights practising at a tilting post, a combat between two wild men and, most remarkable of all, the beautifully drawn birds, illustrate Siferwas's fondness for the anecdotal and his intimate observation of the world of nature.

PLATE 29

THE SHERBORNE MISSAL

Alnwick Castle, Collection of the Duke of Northumberland
533 x 380 mm.

p. 276   *The Mass for Trinity Sunday*

*T*his is one of the most elaborate pages in the *Temporale*. Its theme is *the Celestial Hierarchy*, with *the Trinity*, the subject of the mass, confined to the diagrammatic shield held by the angel in the small Collect initial. The Almighty is depicted in the main initial, surrounded by angels with four elders below flanking the Lamb of God. The borders and column between the texts contain, in addition to Siferwas's characteristic "portrait" heads, representatives of eight of the nine Orders of Angels: *Cherubim, Seraphim, Dominations, Principalities, Powers, Virtues, Angels* and *Archangels*. Each group is represented in a particular fashion: the archangels, with their gold wings covering their bodies, are particularly eye-catching. The tabernacle in the left border, which has been trimmed, shows that Siferwas was familiar with goldsmiths' designs. It contains iconography similar to its counterpart in Plate 28. *Christ in Majesty* is in the center, with the Holy Spirit in the form of a dove over a chalice on an altar in the upper compartment. Below Christ are Bishop Mitford and Abbot Bruyning. *The Four Evangelists* stand in the outer niches, and once again scribe and artist face each other across the stem.

PLATE 30

THE SHERBORNE MISSAL

Alnwick Castle, Collection of the Duke of Northumberland
533 x 380 mm.

p. 47   *The Mass of the Circumcision*

*B*y comparison with the two pages illustrated in the previous plates, the decoration here is restrained. Preparations for the circumcision of Christ (Luke, Chapter II v. 21) are pictured in the main initial, and the altar suggests that the rite is taking place in the temple. The Child is held by the Virgin as the priest tests the sharpness of his knife with his finger. Three doves or pigeons are in Joseph's basket; according to the gospel (Luke, Chapter II v. 24) two doves or pigeons were the offering made during the presentation of Christ in the temple, an event which followed His circumcision and the purification of the Virgin. The wording of the couplet on the scroll held by the angel over the initial is similar to some verses formerly in the chapter-house of Worcester Cathedral, where they were more correctly applied to *the Presentation in the Temple*. In the Collect initial is a profile bust of Siferwas clad as usual in his Dominican habit. Unlike the other representations of the artist in the missal, this is believed to be a realistic, rather than idealized, self-portrait: the physiognomy bears a strong likeness to the large-scale portrait of Siferwas in *The Lovell Lectionary* (Figure XVI). The text on his scroll refers to his patron saint, John the Evangelist, who is adjacent. Siferwas uses scrolls frequently, not simply to bear texts but also as a design feature. Here they are employed most effectively, drawing together the various elements in the decoration of the page. Abbot Bruyning and his guardian angel in the lower left corner are linked with the upper part of the left border by the scroll held in their hands, and they are connected with the figures of John Whas and his angel by the text intertwining through the lower border. The circuit is completed by the long scroll commemorating Whas's patron saint, John the Baptist, which terminates near the feet of the angel at the top of the page. The *vignette* of two hounds pursuing a hare, a fox and a stoat at the end of the lower border is reminiscent of the decoration in England manuscripts of the early years of the fourteenth century.

Column 1

In circumcisio
ne dni. officiu.
[P]uer natus est
nobis 7 filius
datus est nobis
cuius imperiu
sup humerium eius 7 uocabit nome
eius magni consilij angelus. Mul
tiplicabit eius imperiu 7 pacis non
erit finis. oro
nobis nati saluato
ris diem celebrare co
cedis octauum. fac nos quis ci
ptua diuinitate mimiri. cu
ius sumus carnali commercio
reparati. Qui tecu. Lco epi. lec. ad
ro̅e: Apparuit gracia
dei saluatoris nrm.
nobis omnibz homini
bus erudiens nos: ut abne
gantes impietatem 7 secula
ria desideria sobrie 7 iuste et
pie uiuamus in hoc seculo.
Expectantes beatam spem et
aduentum glorie magni dei:
et saluatoris nri ihu xpi. Qui
dedit semetipsum pro nobis
ut nos redimeret ab omni in
iquitate: 7 mundaret sibi po
pulum acceptabilem: sectato
rem bonox operu. Hec loque
re: 7 exortare. In xpo ihu: dn̅o

Column 2

nostro. S. Viderunt omnes fines
terre salutare dei nri iubilate deo omnis
terra. No tum fecit dns salutare su
um ante conspectum gentium reuela
uit iusticiam suam. All.a. Dies
sanctificatus illuxit nobis uenite gen
tes 7 adorate dnm quia hodie descen
dit lux magna sup terram. Sequen.
este 7 incorrupte pange.
uius iubila marie que
sine corpore 7 peperit xpm
inmacula. Eloquia credula suscipies
angelica. hodie sidera mellifluia per
soluunt deo cantici. Iterum omnia
sunt podita uidentium uaticinia. Er
go deo grauida noua dat seculo mira
cula. Maiestas omnifici latet inter
claustra teneritima. Iam edifici po
testas atp natura. Dolens agnina
reddite gratie celestia surpiendo de
prauata. Bon auriflua precoptuit
placita. Et uirginea elegit membra
cristifico nitore delectabilia. Exulta
iam cundida mater 7 sponsa caret 7 p
fecti columba. Virgula diuitici cui
florida numquam marcescit psalmia.
Excelsa sup sidera uirgo sola stu
pent astra matutina te superi uene
rerur luminaria. Miseri tremunt
tartarei catto pedem quam ceperit
amisisti ex qua nci sathan corru
pit primordia. Va et euia mater

PLATE 31

THE BEAUFORT/BEAUCHAMP HOURS

London, British Library, Ms. Royal 2 A.XVIII
216 x 153 mm.

fol. 7v   *Saint John of Bridlington*

*T*he history of this manuscript was first elucidated by Margaret Rickert, who showed that it comprises two separate volumes. Fols. 25-241 consist of a book of hours executed in the late 1430's or early 1440's, almost certainly for Margaret Beauchamp of Bletsoe, wife of John Beaufort, first Duke of Somerset. His obit (he died on May 27, 1444) was added to the calendar, which also contains entries concerning the children of Margaret's two marriages, her Grandison ancestors, and her grandson Henry Tudor (later Henry VII). This part of the manuscript takes its name from her patronage. Its miniatures and initials can be attributed to William Abell and his workshop (see Plate 40).

The first part of Royal 2 A.XVIII, fols. 3-24, dates from the first decade of the fifteenth century and was detached from a psalter now in Rennes (Bibliothèque Muncipale, Ms. 22), the original patron of which is unknown. During the late fifteenth century this psalter was in the possession of Henry Holand, Duke of Exeter and Earl of Huntingdon, and his wife Anne, daughter of Richard, Duke of York. The name *Huntyngdon* occurs at the top of fol. 188v in the Rennes portion and to its calendar have been added the birth dates of five of Duke Richard's children. These entries could not have been made before 1461, for in them Edward IV, one of the children, is designated as king. The entries also include the birth of Anna, daughter of Anne and Henry Holand, who was born in that year.

The decoration of this section of Royal 2 A.XVIII consists of twelve full-page miniatures (fols. 3v-19v) of single saints and a miniature (fol. 23v) of *the Annunciation* with two kneeling patrons (Plate 32). The twelve full-page miniatures are by the so-called "Master of the Beaufort Saints," a Flemish artist whose work can be seen in several English manuscripts. The depiction of *Saint John of Bridlington* is one of his finest achievements. This saint was born in 1320 at Thwing in Yorkshire. After studying at Oxford he returned to his native county and entered the Augustinian priory at Bridlington, eventually became prior and died there in 1379 of the plague. Even during his lifetime he was much revered and steps were immediately taken to have him canonized. This took place in 1401 and three years later his relics were translated into a shrine. This miniature of the saint in the habit of an Augustinian canon is one of the few surviving representations of him in medieval art.

As with the other full-page miniatures in this manuscript by "the Master of the Beaufort Saints," the figure and the enclosing canopy and side-shafts are pasted onto the page. The joins are concealed on three sides by the gold framing and at the top by foliate sprays painted over them. The name *brydlingto* is just discernible in these sprays, serving as a guide for the person pasting the miniature onto the page.

The rather thick paint is applied broadly, but what is lacking in smooth finish is compensated for by the impression of liveliness. The artist's fondness for strongly contrasting colors is well demonstrated.

PLATE 32

THE BEAUFORT/BEAUCHAMP HOURS

London, British Library, Ms. Royal 2 A.XVIII
216 x 153 mm.
fol. 23v   *The Annunciation*

*T*he attribution of this miniature is disputed. Miss Rickert claimed that it was the work of Hand A in *The Carmelite Missal* (Plate 27), and with its facing text-page was originally a portable votive diptych executed before 1400. A few years later, when the full-page miniatures of the saints were painted (Plate 31), *the Annunciation* and its facing text-page were incorporated into the manuscript. Whether or not it was originally part of *The Rennes Psalter, the Annunciation* can more convincingly be assigned to Herman Scheerre.

The scene takes place within a Gothic architectural framework, related in design to those used by "the Master of the Beaufort Saints." In the blue roundel at the upper left, God the Father, surrounded by angels, directs the Holy Ghost to the Virgin. She turns from her devotional reading toward Gabriel whose long spiraling scroll bears a paraphrase of Luke, Chapter I v. 28 ("Hail, thou that art highly favored, the Lord is with thee: blessed art thou among women"). The haloes of Gabriel and the Virgin have bidding prayers asking for their intercession. The kneeling man and woman, presumably the original owners or patrons of the manuscript, are smaller than the Virgin and Gabriel and, placed outside the chapel, merely observe the sacred scene as spectators, not participants. The green cloth covering the Virgin's prie-dieu bears the textual trademark of the artist, Herman Scheerre: *Omnia: levia sunt amanti: si quis amat: non laborat* ("All is easy for one who loves: he who loves toils not"). This is followed by the words *de daer,* which have not so far been interpreted satisfactorily.

The colors and color combinations used by the artist are exquisite. The blue of the roundel containing God the Father and of the Virgin's mantle, the red of the vaulting and of the draperies covering the prie-dieux of the patrons, and the pink of their robes and of Gabriel's, draw the compositional elements together. The balance and harmony, the subtle touches such as the delicate shadows cast on the tiled floor by the Virgin and the Angel, and the serenity of *the Annunciation* in *The Beaufort/Beauchamp Hours* place it firmly among the masterpieces of English medieval painting.

PLATE 33

THE PSALTER AND HOURS OF JOHN, DUKE OF BEDFORD

London, British Library, Ms. Additional 42131
407 x 279 mm.

fol. 73   *Psalm 1. Tree of Jesse and Anointing of David*

John, Duke of Bedford (1389-1435), brother of Henry V and Regent of France from 1422 until his death, owned three of the most lavishly decorated manuscripts executed in the early fifteenth century. Two of them, *The Bedford Hours* (London, British Library, Ms. Additional 18850) and *The Salisbury Breviary* (Paris, Bibliothèque Nationale, Ms. Lat. 17294) were illuminated in France (almost certainly in Paris) by the so-called "Bedford Master" and his associates. The present manuscript, by contrast, was executed in England. The inscription in a line-ending on fol. 21, *I comminde me un to yow. I pray god saue ye duke of bedford,* shows that the manuscript must postdate 1414, when John was created Duke of Bedford. A possible indication that the decoration had not been completed before 1420 is provided by the initial to *Psalm 80,* depicting a royal wedding (Plate 34B): this may be a reference to the marriage in that year of Henry V and Catherine of Valois. The illumination was probably finished before 1423, when the Duke married his first wife, Anne of Burgundy, daughter of John the Fearless, because only his arms are represented (fol. 75), not those of his Duchess. Subsequently the volume passed into the possession of William Catesby (d. 1485), the trusted councillor of Richard III. His arms, either singly or impaling those of his wife Margaret, daughter of William Lord Zouche of Harringworth, occur on fols. 7, 73, 95, 109, 122, 135, 151v, 166v, 183.

The illumination consists of eighteen large historiated initials to the canonical Hours, the Office of the Dead and the psalm divisions, as well as more than two hundred and eighty smaller historiated initials, most containing single "portrait" heads. It was executed primarily in the workshop of Herman Scheerre, who is identified in two line-fillings, *herman your meke seruant* (fol. 124) and *I am herman youre owne seruant* (fol. 232v). Scheerre's own hand executed the initials on fols. 7, 46, 151v (Plate 34B) and 183. Those on the page illustrated here and on fol. 95 (Plate 34A) are by an artist who, although close to Scheerre in figure-style, was influenced by the landscape innovations of "the Boucicaut Master" and his followers in France.

The page depicted here is the first of the psalms, *Beatus vir. The Anointing of David* in the initial is a subject more commonly found illustrating *Psalm 26* in English fourteenth- and fifteenth-century psalters. The iconography follows the Biblical text (I Samuel, Chapter XVI vv. 12-13), and shows Jesse presenting David, his youngest son, to Samuel. The aged prophet, following the instructions of God the Father, who appears outside the initial in the upper left corner, anoints David with a horn of oil. The three figures are set against a rocky landscape and a starry sky. The tops of the rocks and the sky lighten towards the horizon, a means of representing spatial recession borrowed by this artist from "the Boucicaut Master." The facial features in this initial are softly modeled, as is Jesse's sleeping figure in the lower border. From his side springs the vine containing busts of his descendants, the Old Testament Kings, and near the top of the right border, the Virgin. The border figures, including God the Father and the angels at the corners, are not by the artist who executed the initial and the reclining Jesse. From the five figures in the right border spring foliate sprays which encircle the crest, shield of arms and devices of John, Duke of Bedford. The shield in the lower margin bears the arms of William Catesby and his wife.

Eatus uir qui
non abijst i con
silio impiorū:
et in uia pecca
torum non ste
tit. et in cathed
pestilencie non
sedit. Sed in
lege domini uoluntas eius: et in lege ei
meditabitur die ac nocte. Et erit tan
qm lignum quod plantatum est secus
decursus aquarum: quod fructū suum
dabit in tempore suo. Et folium eius
non defluet: et omnia quecunq; faciet
prosperabuntur. Non sic impij non
sic: sed tanquam puluis quem proicit
uentus a facie terre. Ideo non resur
gunt impij in iudicio: neq; peccatores in

PLATE 34

THE PSALTER AND HOURS OF JOHN, DUKE OF BEDFORD

London, British Library, Ms. Additional 42131
407 x 279 mm.
A. fol. 95   *Initial introducing Psalm 26*

The initial D frames the illustration of I Samuel, Chapter XVII vv. 34-36: "And David said unto Saul, Thy servant kept his father's sheep, and there came a lion and a bear, and took a lamb out of the flock. And I went out after him, and smote him, and delivered it out of his mouth: and when he arose against me, I caught him by his beard, and smote him, and slew him. Thy servant slew both the lion and the bear." The only non-Biblical embellishment introduced into the initial is the unicorn lying dead in the background. The impression of spatial depth created by the receding landscape is slightly negated by the delicately diapered background. The same artist also painted *the Anointing of David* (Plate 33).

B. fol. 151v   *Initial introducing Psalm 80*

The iconography of this initial is of particular significance in dating the manuscript. The subject is the sixth in the cycle of scenes from the life of David, and depicts his marriage to Saul's daughter Michal (I Samuel, Chapter XVIII v. 27). It is not part of the usual series of psalter illustrations and is, moreover, rarely represented in medieval art. The most plausible explanation for its presence in *The Bedford Psalter and Hours* is that it alludes to the wedding which took place on 2 June 1420 between Catherine of Valois and Henry V of England, brother of John, Duke of Bedford.

This initial can be attributed to Herman Scheerre. In contrast with the two miniatures illustrated above and in Plate 33, there is no attempt to create perspective or spatial depth.

The initials on fols. 109, 122 and 135 are the work of the French-influenced assistant. The third main illuminator, who was responsible for the Passion initials on fols. 12v, 21v, 24v, 26v, 28, 30, 33 and 37, was a member of the Johannes workshop and may have been the assistant who worked with him on *The Hours of Elizabeth the Queen*.

me t miserere mei. Des r
ducto: in ecclesijs bndicar
Onu
natu
mea

techo
quo
prant sup me nocentes: ut
meas. Qut tribulant n
tuam t salut erimus.

Buccinate i neomenia
die solennitatis vie

PLATE 35

"LI ROMANS DU BOIN ROI ALEXANDRE" AND MARCO POLO "LI LIVRES DU GRAUNT CAAM"

Oxford, Bodleian Library, Ms. Bodley 264
410 x 284 mm.

fol. 2v   Frontispiece to *Li Romans du Boin Roi Alexandre*

*T*he major part of this volume (fols. 1-208) consists of *The Romance of Alexander* written in Picard dialect in 1338. Its decoration was completed on 18 April 1344 by the Flemish illuminator Jehans de Grise. By the opening years of the fifteenth century the manuscript had found its way to England, where a further *Alexander* episode (fols. 209-215v) and the *Marco Polo* text (fols. 218-271v) were added, the former in a West Midlands dialect, the latter in French. Although attempts have been made to associate the volume with Thomas of Woodstock, Duke of Gloucester (d. 1397), whose library at Pleshy included three books on the life of Alexander, the first known owner is Richard Woodville, Lord Rivers, father-in-law of Edward IV. According to an inscription on fol. 274 he purchased the manuscript in London on 1 January 1466.

The *Marco Polo* is illustrated with thirty-eight miniatures, from the workshop of an artist, Johannes, who wrote *Johannes me fecit* on the hem of the Grand Caam on fol. 220. He seems to have had at least two assistants, one poor and the other of a talent approaching his own.

The frontispiece to the *Alexander* is contemporary with the *Marco Polo* cycle and it has been suggested that it replaced a damaged original frontispiece of 1338-44. Four episodes from the early life of Alexander the Great (356-323 B.C.), based on the late twelfth-century text by Alexandre de Paris, are pictured. The first scene (upper left) shows the birth of Alexander. His mother Olympias, sitting up in bed, is about to take the child wrapped in swaddling clothes from a midwife. A second female attendant proffers a gold cup. A third midwife is heating a pot over an open fire — a charming domestic touch. The male figure on the right is the sorcerer Nectanebus, last king of Egypt; according to the legend Alexander was born when Nectanebus had finished calculating the stars of heaven. The second scene is the presentation of the young prince Alexander by his father Philip II of Macedon to the group of courtiers, which again includes Nectanebus. The third episode represents Alexander's dream: the prince lies asleep with a serpent on the bed beside him while King Philip points out his son and the serpent to a group of three attendants, one of whom may be Nectanebus. The final scene is of the taming of Bucephalus. Alexander hammers on the door of the stable where Bucephalus, represented here as a unicorn, lies on the floor strewn with bones of his human victims. The color combinations, with pink, green, blue and red predominating, are the same as those employed by Johannes in his miniatures to the *Marco Polo*. The treatment of faces in the frontispiece is less subtle. The thick contour lines, less careful modeling and coarser treatment of hair and beards suggests that although the original page design was the work of Johannes, the painting was executed in collaboration with an assistant.

PLATE 36

THE HOURS OF ELIZABETH THE QUEEN
London, British Library, Ms. Additional 50001
216 x 152 mm.
fol. 7   *The Last Supper*

Although the original recipient of this volume, which dates from *c.* 1420-30, has not been identified, it subsequently passed through the hands of a distinguished series of owners. Of these, the first appears to have been Cecily, wife of Henry Beauchamp, Duke of Warwick between 1445 and 1446 (Plates 38, 39), inasmuch as her death (in 1450) is recorded in an erased inscription on fol. 147. Some time between 1487 and 1509 the volume came into the possession of Elizabeth, daughter of Edward IV, who married Henry VII in 1486 and was crowned Queen the following year. Her signature, *Elysabeth ye quene,* appears on fol. 22. From Elizabeth it passed to her cousin, Edward Stafford, Duke of Buckingham, who was beheaded in 1521; his erased signature is on fol. 152.

The decoration consists of eighteen half-page miniatures, mostly of the Passion, numerous initials (the majority of which contain "portrait" heads) and fine borders. They appear to be the work of two artists, the better of whom is the Johannes who signed the *Marco Polo* text added to the *Alexander Romance* (Plate 35). The second illuminator was an assistant with a style very similar to that of the Passion miniatures in *The Bedford Psalter and Hours,* which in turn are closely related iconographically to *The Hours of Elizabeth the Queen.*

The decoration of the page shown here is by Johannes. Although Passion cycles quite frequently replace scenes from the Life of the Virgin as illustrations to Books of Hours, the choice of *the Last Supper* as a preface to the text for Matins is exceptional. The moment depicted is the revelation of Judas Iscariot as Christ's betrayer. Christ is seated in the center, flanked by St. Peter and St. Paul (the latter identified by his bald head). Lying asleep on Christ's chest is the youthful St. John, an image taken from his gospel (John, Chapter XIII vv. 23, 25). Christ raises His hand as He speaks; the gesture of horror made by St. Paul and the manner in which the Apostles gaze at one another clearly illustrate their reactions to the revelation of the coming betrayal. Judas is seated at the corner of the bench on the right. In Matthew, Chapter XXVI v. 23, and Mark, Chapter XIV v. 20, he shows himself as the traitor by dipping his hand into the same dish as Christ. In this miniature Judas is trying to conceal under the tablecloth a fish he has taken from the dish in front of Christ. The motif of Judas hiding the fish, which is found occasionally from the twelfth century onwards, appears to be based upon his thieving tendencies, mentioned in John, Chapter XII v. 6. A very similar example occurs in the east window of Great Malvern Priory Church, Worcestershire, executed at about the same time. The architectural framework of this miniature provides a stylistic connection with the medium of stained glass: the small prophets set in niches are very reminiscent of early fifteenth-century glazing in the Minster and parish churches of York.

PLATE 37

GEOFFREY CHAUCER: "TROILUS AND CRISEYDE"

Cambridge, Corpus Christi College, Ms. 61
315 x 222 mm.
fol. 1v   *Frontispiece: Chaucer reciting his poem*

*H*ad the decoration of this book been completed, it would have been the most lavishly illuminated English medieval secular text known. Spaces were left for ninety illustrations to the text proper, in addition to the frontispiece. However, only the latter was executed. This is separated into two parts by rocks running in a shallow diagonal line. The upper scene depicts the meeting of two processions of elegantly dressed lords and ladies, one winding down from a castle perched high on a rocky peak, the other emerging from a multi-turreted castle. Below the rocks a public recital is taking place. Their costume suggests that the audience is composed of people of high rank. The reciter is undoubtedly Geoffrey Chaucer, and it can be assumed that he is reciting the *Troilus*. The once-popular theory that the frontispiece represents Chaucer reciting his poem to Richard II and his Court, and that historical personages (including the king himself) can be identified, is now discounted.

No other illumination by this artist has been recognized to date. He was undoubtedly one of the best exponents in England of the International Gothic style. The graceful courtly figures, dressed in the highest fashion, and the fairy-tale setting with its gold background are the quintessence of the refined aristocratic art of the early fifteenth century. The border foliage and the leaves and sprays in the margins suggest that the illuminator was an Englishman; the rocky landscape with the castles points to his acquaintance with the work of "the Boucicaut Master" in France.

Chaucer is believed to have completed the *Troilus* around 1385, and this manuscript appears on paleographical and art-historical grounds to date from the first quarter of the fifteenth century. Its earliest known owner is the literary entrepreneur and commentator on Chaucer's minor poems, John Shirley (*c.* 1366-1456); the first of two English couplets added on fol. 1 is in his hand.

PLATE 38

THE PSALTER AND HOURS OF HENRY BEAUCHAMP, EARL OF WARWICK

New York, Pierpont Morgan Library, Ms. M. 893
273 x 186 mm.
fol. 12   *The Annunciation*

*T*his Book of Hours and Psalter, of Sarum Use, was made for Henry Beauchamp, Earl (subsequently Duke) of Warwick. His signature *Warrewyk* and motto *Deservyng causeth* occur at the base of fol. 12. Henry Beauchamp succeeded as Earl in 1439 and died in 1446, which provides a quite precise dating for the manuscript. By 1482 it had found its way to Italy, where five half-page miniatures were added by North Italian artists.

Two artists were responsible for the original decoration, comprised of twenty-two miniatures. The first executed the pages illustrated in this and the following plate. The second artist, who used stronger coloring and more angular drapery-fold conventions, has been identified as William Abell.

In common with *The Hours of Elizabeth the Queen* (Plate 36), the Hours of the Virgin in this manuscript are illustrated by scenes of Christ's Passion. The only exception is Matins, which is preceded by *the Annunciation*. Even here there is an allusion to the Passion in the form of the Christ Child traveling down the rays emanating from God the Father towards the Virgin: the Child is holding a tau-cross, emphasizing His redeeming sacrifice for mankind. Apart from this, the essential iconography and composition of *the Annunciation* scene differ little from that of *The Beaufort/Beauchamp Hours* (Plate 32). The illuminator too, though lacking the delicacy and refinement of Scheerre, conforms to the canons of the International Gothic style.

As is usual in books of hours the border decoration of the opening page for Matins is more lavish than elsewhere in the manuscript. Some delightful birds are among the delicate sprays and flowers in the right margin.

PLATE 39

THE PSALTER AND HOURS OF HENRY BEAUCHAMP, EARL OF WARWICK

New York, Pierpont Morgan Library, Ms. M. 893
273 x 186 mm.

fol. 127v   *Psalm 26*

*T*his is the second in a series of eight miniatures concerned with King David which mark the main psalm divisions. The leader of the three stocky figures on the left points out to his companions King David and his vision of the Lord. The three observers wear fashionable mid-fifteenth century costumes. As usual David is shown with his harp, probably in direct reference to verse 6 of *Psalm 26* ("I will sing praises unto the Lord").

The figures are in a peaceful pastoral landscape. Sheep, tended by the diminutive shepherd on the right, graze in the foreground and on the nearest grassy hill. Other hills, crowned with trees, walled towns and a windmill, recede into the distance below a sky, the small, scudding silver clouds of which have oxidized. The landscape and high horizon level reveal that this artist, in common with one of the illuminators of *The Bedford Psalter and Hours* (Plates 33, 34A) and the artist of the *Troilus* frontispiece (Plate 37), has absorbed the innovations of "the Boucicaut Master" and his followers. The border decoration betrays no French influence and is typical of that found in English manuscripts of the first half of the fifteenth century.

PLATE 40

THE ABINGDON MISSAL

Oxford, Bodleian Library, Ms. Digby 227
358 x 242 mm.
Volume I, fol. 113v   *The Crucifixion*

This Missal is in two volumes, of which the second is Trinity College, Oxford, Ms. 75. A colophon on fol. 270v records that the manuscript was written in 1461 for William Ashenden, Abbot of the Benedictine monastery of Abingdon between 1435 and 1468. Apart from the full-page *Crucifixion* Digby 227 contains thirteen historiated initials; a further twelve are in Trinity College Ms. 75.

The emphasis in this *Crucifixion* image is on God's sacrifice of His Son for the redemption of the world, a theme directly related to the Mass, and portrays the moment of Christ's death. The star-spangled sky represents the darkness that passed over the world between the sixth and the ninth hours. Christ's eyes are closed and His head lolls to one side; the Holy Ghost, in the form of a dove, appears to be perched on the arm of the cross during its passage towards God the Father who awaits it with a welcoming gesture. The shield held by the angel set among the luxuriant foliage and sprays in the left border is charged with the five wounds of Christ. The long scroll issuing from the figure of the patron, Abbot Ashenden, in the lower left corner, bears a prayer in adoration of Christ. The two shields in the lower border are charged with (left) the arms of Abingdon Abbey and (right) those, it is assumed, of Ashenden. The symbols of the Evangelists are in the corners.

The illumination in *The Abingdon Missal* is considered to be the work of William Abell. His style differs considerably from that of Scheerre, Siferwas and the other International Gothic artists illustrated in preceding plates. The draperies of Abbot Ashenden and the Virgin fall in sharp, angular folds and the solemn, rather unattractive, faces are heavily modeled. The strongly contrasting colors and heavy outlines are characteristic of Abell.